women, islam and cinema

LOCATIONS

series editors:
BARRY CURTIS AND STEPHEN BARBER

LOCATIONS is a new series of thematic books examining contemporary
genres and hybrids in national and international cinema. Each book
contains numerous black and white images and a fresh critical exploration
of aspects of film's relationship with other media, major themes within
film, or different aspects of national film cultures.

on release:

projected cities
STEPHEN BARBER

animals in film
JONATHAN BURT

women, islam and cinema

GÖNÜL DÖNMEZ-COLIN

REAKTION BOOKS

For André

Reaktion Books Ltd
79 Farringdon Road
London ECIM 3JU, UK

www.reaktionbooks.co.uk

First published 2004

Printed and bound in Great Britain by Cromwell Press

British Library Cataloguing in Publication Data

Dönmez-Colin, Gönül
   Women, Islam and cinema. - (Locations)
   1. Motion pictures and women - Islamic countries 2. Women in motion
   pictures 3. Motion picyures - Religous aspects - Islam
   I. Title
   791.4'3'082'091767

ISBN 1 8619 220 9

contents

introduction

The relationship of Islam to cinema is an ambivalent one. Notable Iranian filmmaker Mohsen Makhmalbaf, as a child, refused to talk to his mother for days when he found out that she had gone to the movies. In 1978, during the last year of Mohammad Reza Shah Pahlavi's reign, fundamentalists burned a theatre, killing hundreds of people. Today, in the Islamic Republic of Iran, to be a filmmaker or an actor is an honourable occupation. On the other hand, in secular Turkey, young Anatolian women have been killed in public squares by family members for entering cinema halls. Ironically, both Ayatollah Khomeini, the leader of the Islamic Republic, and Kemal Atatürk, the founder of the Turkish Republic, once praised cinema.

Women's place (or lack of it) in the cinemas of the Islamic countries is directly linked to social and political evolutions in which religion and religious customs play an important role. The Islamic revolution in Iran and the compulsory veiling of women pushed women into the shadow, but eventually stimulated a movement among women to go behind the camera to have their voices heard. Commercial

Turkish cinema's reactionary stance, particularly regarding gender issues, led to two extremely diverse movements, one defending a Marxist point of view and the other an Islamist one.

This book explores the place of women as spectators, images and image constructors in the cinemas of the countries where Islam is the predominant religion. The roles that religious ideology and cultural attitudes towards women play in developing narratives is an integral part of the discussion.

I have focused the book on the cinemas of Iran and Turkey from the Middle East, drawing parallels from Kazakhstan and Uzbekistan, the two Central Asian Republics of the former Soviet Union, and Pakistan, Bangladesh, Malaysia and Indonesia, the prominently Muslim Asian countries with a challenging film industry. Some of the relevant films made in India by and for Muslim Indians are also explored.

Turkey and Iran are the two non-Arab countries in the Middle East that share several common traits, such as history, customs, traditions and religion, and most of these traits are extended to Central Asia. However, Turkey is a secular state, whereas Iran is governed by *sharia*, the divine law. Soviet rule that lasted for over seven decades made some irreversible changes to ancestral ways of life as well as to culture in the Turkic Republics of Central Asia that share a common language family, the Turkic, with Turkey. Now, as part of the Commonwealth of Independent States (CIS), these countries are essentially Muslim and on the road to recovering their Muslim identity.

Pakistan, Bangladesh, Malaysia and Indonesia, on the surface, may not appear to have many common points with the above countries except for religion. The influences of Hinduism in Pakistan and Bangladesh and Buddhism in Malaysia and Indonesia are certainly evident in all forms of art, including cinema. The objective of this book is to find a possible unity in such diversity.

Historical investigations reveal remarkable transnational elements in the way cinema has evolved in these Muslim countries, where it generally began as entertainment for men by men. Turkish women are said to have donned male clothing or dressed as Christians to accompany men into the cinema halls. In 1909, armed fundamentalists occupied a theatre threatening to knife any woman who dared to set foot inside. Special screenings were arranged for women on certain days of the week, and some cinemas divided the halls with a wooden board into *haremlik* and *selamlık*, women on one side and men on the other. According to the memoirs of a cinema owner, Kemal Atatürk was not happy when he noticed that the Ankara theatre where he went to see a film was filled with men while the large crowd of women who cheered him outside was barred from entering. He ordered his aide to let in all women. The film could not start because of the long applause from the women, and that is how the first non-segregated film was watched, in the presence of the leader himself.

The beginnings of Iranian cinema follow a similar pattern in regard to women. Early films were shown in noblemen's houses to segregated audiences. Ordinary men were

Muslim Turkish women appear on screen for the first time in Muhsin Ertuğrul's *Ateşten Gömlek / A Shirt of Fire* (1923)

able to experience cinema in 1908, five years after its arrival in the country, whereas ordinary women had to wait another twenty-one years, until the country's first professional camera-man, Khanbaba Mo'tazedi, opened a movie theatre for women. Traditional and religious circles, none the less, remained strongly against cinema, which they believed advocated Western values and secularism, if not impiety.

Mo'tazedi had to close his cinema after just one year for lack of films to show, but two years later he opened another, which was very successful. When the building was destroyed in a fire, he took the opportunity to suggest that women would feel more secure if men were present. As mixed theatres were out of the question, the issue was resolved by sitting women on the right and men on the left, the *haremlik* and *selamlık* formula of Turkey. Cinema Pari opened under such conditions, and other theatres soon followed suit.

If Muslim women had to wait several years before they could become spectators, they had to wait even longer to become actors. Until the establishment of the secular Turkish Republic in 1923, all female roles were played by Armenians, Greeks and White Russians. When Muhsin Ertuğrul, a foreign-educated theatre director, decided to adapt for the screen an autobiographical novel by the notable woman writer Halide Edip Adıvar, *Ateşten Gömlek / A Shirt of Fire*, about the struggles of a patriotic woman during the war of independence, Adyvar insisted that Turkish women should play the female parts. Permission had to be granted from the husband of Bediha Muvahhid, the lead, and *A Shirt of Fire* became the first Turkish film in which Muslim women took part.

The first Iranian silent feature, *Abi and Rabi* (1930) by Ovanes Ohanian, was a comedy with no women in the cast or the crew. The second Iranian film, *Brother's Revenge* (1931), daringly introduced two women characters but they had to be played by non-Muslims. The third film, *Haji Agha, the Film Star* (1932) by Ohanian, cast an Armenian woman in the lead.

Abdolhossein Sepanta broke the taboo with *Dokhtar-e Lor / The Lor Girl* (1933), the first sound film, which he shot in India, featuring a Muslim woman, Ruhangiz, as a rural girl named Golonar (meaning pomegranate blossom), who sang and danced in tea houses and inns on the Lorestan–Khuzistan road. The film had no connection to Iranian realities of the time, but the heroic tale of a girl surviving on her own attracted the public and *The Lor Girl* was shown simultaneously in two theatres in Tehran for nearly seven months.

In the field of directing, the battle for Muslim women to achieve success in this male dominated profession is far from won. A number of progressive women filmmakers have emerged in Iran in the 1990s despite strict control from the Ministry of Culture and Islamic Guidance. In comparison, the history of Turkish cinema reveals a paucity of women behind the camera. In the former USSR, very few women were able to enter VGIK, the prestigious All-Union State Institute of Cinematography in Moscow that has trained all notable Soviet filmmakers. For the women of Central Asia, where directing is generally considered a man's job, prospects have been exiguous. A handful of women in the profession in Pakistan have produced films matching in violence and sexploitation those of their male colleagues. In Bangladesh, home to a courageous woman writer, Taslima Nasreen, who faced the death penalty for questioning gender injustices committed in the name of religion, the industry has been almost exclusively dominated by men. In Indonesia, women filmmakers have traditionally followed the male point of view but in the 1990s a new generation emerged with a different vision. Of the five producers actively working today, four are women. Their efforts receive extensive support by acclaimed cinematic figures such as Christian Hakim, actor and producer. A similar movement has already started in Malaysia and continues successfully.

Turkey, Iran, Pakistan, Bangladesh, Malaysia and Indonesia saw a proliferation of soft porno films and 'lumpenization' of the screens in the 1970s when political turmoil was at its peak. Such exploitation, which targeted the up-rooted and dispossessed migrant population in large urban areas, ended in Iran with the arrival of the Islamic Revolution and in Turkey with the emergence of *d'auteur* cinema. In Malaysia it continues in a sporadic fashion, whereas in Indonesia it exists mostly in video and digital format. In Pakistan and Bangladesh exploitative commercial cinema is the dominant genre although individual filmmakers searching for a personal expression are beginning to have their voices heard, their search coinciding with the search for a more positive image of women in their countries.

Chapter 1 examines how women are presented within the male-dominated Islamic cinema, exploring common themes, trends and stereotypes with attention to more recent developments. First experiences with the moving images estab-lished certain attitudes towards women that have developed along transnational lines sharing distinct patterns, similar themes, motives and stereotypes. Family is pivotal to films from most Muslim countries, often as a microcosm of the social system, and is instrumental in creating a national identity. Family also functions as a mechanism to merge religious, social and political values through the representation of women in roles defined by their relationships with male figures.

Women are no longer victims, asexual nonentities or sexual objects in majority of contemporary Turkish films. Yet, during a discussion in Istanbul in the spring of 2003, Ali Özgentürk, a prominent voice from the middle generation, defined Turkish cinema as essentially a Muslim cinema that preserves in its subconscious the residues of the Ottoman culture, the foundation of the present Turkish society. Women are defined as good or bad through their sexuality – bad woman makes love, good woman gets married. Good woman is an innocent, asexual icon who does not live. Bad woman's fate is bars and brothels. The language of the body is the language of Islam.

Feminist film critics claim that male visual pleasure is the controlling pleasure. The popularity of rape scenes, particularly in mainstream cinema, provokes a discourse on audience voyeurism. It can also be argued that the inevitable suicide of the rape victim reinforces the cultural myth of patriarchy, which claims that a raped woman is no longer 'pure'. Some films show rape as representing indirect political oppression of men who are linked through an unequal power relationship with the rapist(s). Chapter 2 examines examples of violence against women, and particularly rape, in the cinemas of Turkey, Pakistan and Malaysia, trying to understand its meaning and purpose for the audience and the filmmaker.

Cinema with a strong religious ideology drew attention in Turkey in the 1990s as *white cinema* when Islamist parties began to gain political prominence. *White cinema* had its roots in a similar movement that had created controversy in the 1970s under the banner of *milli cinema* (national cinema) and, like its antecedent, has remained essentially marginal. In India, *Muslim socials,* advocating moral and religious values, were very popular in the 1960s as family entertainment. A distinctively Islamist cinema adhering to *feqh*-based ideology (Islamic jurisprudence) was promoted in Iran during the First Republic following the 1979 Islamic revolution and lasted until the mid-1980s. Chapter 3 examines these three different movements, occurring in different periods, whose common ground is the messages they purport to convey to women.

Dariush Mehrjui from Iran, Atıf Yılmaz from Turkey and Ermek Shinarbaev from Kazakhstan have consistently made films focusing on women's issues in a world dominated by men. Widowhood, endorsed polygamy, male-child syndrome, female sexuality and sexual emancipation are the specific concerns of these films. However, to label these works as 'women's films' in the Hollywood sense of the word would be limiting. The protagonists may be women but the pivotal issues do not exist without men. Customs, traditions and dogmatic religious practices still regulate lives in many parts of the world, affecting both sexes equally. Hence, the emancipation of women is also a release for men. Chapter 4 views the approaches of these male filmmakers to the problem of women and compares their points of view with those of notable women filmmakers: Rakhshan Bani-Etemad and Tahmineh Milani from Iran, Bilge Olgaç from Turkey and Kamara Kamalova from Uzbekistan. Questions are raised as to the 'gaze' and whether there are marked differences in the depiction of women when women are behind the camera.

The subject of women has always been controversial in post-revolutionary Iranian cinema and is often used by the authorities in defining borders. The election of moderate Mohammad Khatami as president in 1997 and his re-election in 2001 has led to a relative relaxation of censorship laws encouraging the young generation to voice their concerns openly about the closed Islamic society and its treatment of women. Chapter 5 focuses on some of the best examples of this dynamic New Iranian Cinema, which reflects women's plight in a period of transition when modernity and contemporaneity challenge the traditional values of Islam.

Considering the diversity of cultures, rather than viewing national cinemas as aspects of a single development, I have focused on individual histories, traditions and social and economical circumstances as points of reference. These points are examined in the context of social and political evolution and the status of women within Islam, keeping in mind that there are different types of Islam depending on time and place and that the situation of women in Islamic countries is not homogeneous. I have tried to maintain an exploratory approach considering the multifold and evolutionary nature of the subject.

The African continent, where other factors beside religion strongly shape attitudes and points of view, is beyond the scope of this book. Two other factors have influenced this decision: Black Africa's film production is presently rather limited and Arab cinema is already well documented. The countries I have chosen, although rich in cinematic history, are not well known in the West – except perhaps Iran, which has enjoyed recent attention. My objective is to look at the cinema of the 'other' and meet the challenge of discovering less known territories.

Edward Said remarked that 'Given the present circumstances, with neither "Islam" nor "the West" at peace with each other or with themselves, it may seem exceptionally futile to ask whether, for members of one culture, knowledge of other cultures is really possible.'[1] Having been brought up in one culture and having matured in the other, I have taken the liberty to stand both inside and outside. Investigating the interrelation of women and cinema in the context of Islamic culture has been a challenge for me. Misconceptions do exist, most of which stem from lack of information. The purpose of this book is to arrive at a better understanding of exactly what is 'inside the frame' regarding women in Islamic cinema.

1 representations of women

. . . And women
our women
with their horrific and blessed hands
*   delicate little chins, grand eyes*
*   our mothers*
*   wives, sweethearts,*
and dying as if never lived
and the place of who at our table
*   second to our cow*
and with whom we elope to the mountains,
*   for whom we serve in prison,*
and in the harvest, tobacco, firewood and the market
and tied to the plough
and in the stall
in the glare of knives thrust into the earth
with their playful heavy hips and cymbals, ours
*   women*
*   our women.*

Nazım Hikmet [1]

The subject of women has occupied cinema since its invention. About half of the first fiction films made before the foundation of the Turkish Republic in 1923 were about women, love and marriage, as a glance at some of the titles reveals: *Hikmet Ağanın İzdivacı / The Marriage of Hikmet Aga* (1918), *Mürebbiye / The Governess* (1919) and *Binnaz* (1919). Whether the characters were well developed, realistic and/or fair is another matter.

In Turkey, where some restaurants still advertise themselves as *aile lokantası* (family restaurant where single men are not allowed), there is a definite distinction between *aile kadını* (the family woman) and the woman who experiments freely with her sexuality, who is often regarded as *fahişe* (the prostitute). The latter was the fascination of Turkish cinema right from the start. The *tawaif,* the courtesan of the Mughal culture, presented with delicate euphemism in several classic films from Muslim India, carries, in essence, the same characteristics as the *fahişe* and shares the same fate. In Indonesian films, next to the wife and the daughter, *ca bau kan,* the prostitute, is the most common role for women.

'Prostitution seems to have been simply a complement to marriage in the first place', writes Georges Bataille in his seminal work, *Eroticism*:

A transitional step, the transgression in the marriage ceremony, led to an organized daily life, and labour could be shared between husband and wife. A transgression of this sort was no way of consecrating

Binnaz (1919) by
Ahmet Fehim

anyone to erotic life. Sexual relations continued overtly and the transgression that initiated them was not stressed after the first contact. With prostitution, the prostitute was dedicated to a life of transgression. The sacred or forbidden aspect of sexual activity remained apparent in her, for her whole life was dedicated to violating the taboo.[2]

The first 'fallen women' of Turkish cinema are the two heroes of Sedat Simavi's provocative *Pençe / The Clutch* (1917), a film that praises free love. Leman is presented as a woman with an insatiable appetite for men and Feride is an adulteress. They are followed by Angelique, an 'amoral' French beauty in Ahmet Fehim's sex vaudeville, *Mürebbiye / The Governess* (1919) who seduces all men in a rich household. This, incidentally, is the first Turkish film to show a woman in her intimate attire and the first to be censored. The commandant of the occupying French forces banned the film for showing a French woman as immoderately sexy, disregarding Fehim's

Şehvet Kurbanı /
The Victim of Lust
by Muhsin Ertuğrul
(1939)

argument that *Mürebbiye* represented the silent resistance of an artist to the foreign occupation.

Muhsin Ertuğrul, who found *Pençe* shameful, made his own version of a 'fallen woman' with *Istanbulda Bir Facia-i Aşk / A Love Tragedy in Istanbul* (1922), based on the life of the notorious *Şişli Güzeli Mediha Hanım*, a beautiful seductress from the Şişli upper-class neighbourhood, who was murdered by one of her desperate lovers. The film started the tradition of 'bad woman' films that showed how urban *petit bourgeois* males who were destroyed by their passions recovered their self-esteem through twists and turns of the plot. The happy ending was essential to such formula films, which often included murders, false accusations and loss of memory. The genre became so popular that the same recipe was repeated in countless films of the next four decades.

Ertuğrul continued his 'fallen woman' theme into the 1930s, adding some spice with stories of high society scandals involving rich skirt-chasers. He produced some classics along the way, and with *Şehvet Kurbanı / The Victim of Lust* (1939), inspired by *Der Blauer Engel / The Blue Angel,* Turkish cinema found its own Marlene Dietrich in the sensual Cahide Sonku, the first woman to introduce eroticism to Turkish cinema. Sonku was very successful in the role of a mysterious temptress, although her blonde hair and European appearance appealed mostly to the educated middle-class urbanite.

The women in these early films were not actually prostitutes since they did not have sex for money. Rather, they were seductresses with 'loose morals' and a sexual appetite that was interpreted as nymphomania, a convenient subject of amusement as well as fodder for the fantasies of men from a closed society, the largest part of the audience. Family women were absent mainly because films that depicted them as shameless adventurers or coquettish seducers were against their concepts of morality.

The vamp was appropriated by Turkish cinema in the 1960s as an extension of the prostitute. The erotic accessories of Leyla Sayar, the most famous vamp, evoked fetishism and catered to sado-masochistic fantasies. In *Şehrazat-Dişi Örümcek / Scheherazade – The Female Spider* (1964), she was the praying mantis who cruised bars and killed men after a night of sex until she found her true love.

Naturally, the vamp is not indigenous to Muslim cinema, its archetypal representations including Delilah, Cleopatra, Carmen and Salome among others. Stories of temptresses who feed off the foundations of society and lure men to their destruction go back to the early years of Hollywood. The vamp uses her sexuality to manipulate men for her devious aims. She can destroy their masculinity as represented in society by leading them to excesses that may result in loss of social status, and in financial and emotional insecurity. The popularity of the genre in traditional Muslim societies finds an explanation in the need to preserve family values, as the vamp often pays with her life for her transgressions.

Both prostitute and vamp films traditionally show societal pressures as reasons for women to turn to 'bad ways'. These range from losing her virginity through weakness or rape to the death of her husband or the desertion of her lover. Left without an owner, the woman is prey to evil. She may not be responsible for her 'fall', but that does not alter the stigma attached to the profession. The woman is merchandise to be bought and sold, and those who receive their share of the *sermaye* (capital, but also prostitute in Turkish slang) are men. They reap the benefits without dire consequences. Commercial cinema endorses the contention of the patriarchal Muslim society that prostitutes are a disgrace and a threat to respectable family life. The choices left to such women are either to accept their fate or to find salvation in death. The third option is to repent and embrace Islam. In Halit Refiğ's *Kurtar Beni / Save Me* (1987), Ayten enters the mosque, discovers the true path to Allah and marries Salih, the *imam*.

According to Atıf Yılmaz, in a capitalist system where everyone exploits each other and men exploit women, prostitutes cannot be saved unless they do to others what is done to them. In *Asiye Nasıl Kurtulur? / How Can Asiye Be Saved?* (1986), Asiye follows in the steps of her mother and becomes a 'fallen woman'. Then a rich client suddenly dies leaving behind a bag full of money. If, as an honourable citizen she gave the money to the man's wife or to the police, she would be back where she came from. She keeps the money and continues, with determination and patience, the profession she knows best, not forgetting to exploit those weaker than her. This is how she is saved!

Fahişe and *vamp* cycles dominated Yeşilçam (Turkish commercial cinema) until the 1970s. Except for one or two serious works, the characters in these films were totally unbelievable. Neither the directors nor the actors were familiar with the milieu of bars, prostitutes and brothels. However, the producers continued to bank on the double advantage of films that conveniently legalized women's naked bodies and sex on screen, catering to male fantasies, and at the same time sent a moral lesson to the chaste family woman, as 'bad women' always received the punishment they deserved. The genre gained a new dimension in the 1970s with talented newcomers, such as Ömer Kavur and Yılmaz Güney, who approached sexuality from the perspective of the individual. By the mid-1980s, with social and economical changes in the status of women, the theme of women who fall when left without an owner became obsolete.

India produces over 900 films a year. The thrust of the commercial cinema is to represent Indian society as one uniform culture, the Hindu. However, the rich literary tradition of Urdu culture has on several occasions infiltrated into cinema, creating some masterpieces through historical renditions of the Mughal culture of romantic poetry, music and dance, which flourished in the *kotha*, the house of the *tawaif*, the dancer-singer-prostitute. Zubeida (1911–1990), born a Muslim princess, is perhaps the first actor to establish the 'innocent' courtesan roles in big Urdu costume films. The tradition extended to Meena Kumari (1933–1972), who had made her fame in the roles of self-sacrificing wife and mother. With *Pakeezah / The Pure One* (1971) by Kamal Amrohi, she perfected the image of the melancholic object of fantasy.

Except for the euphemism that conventions dictate, the *tawaif* figure is similar to the *fahişe*. The *kotha* separates the woman of pleasure from the chaste and obedient wife in the Indian Muslim social order. While the simple wife is enslaved inside the home, the husband looks for sophisticated companionship and erotic dalliance in the woman set apart from society for that purpose. Liaison with a *tawaif* is shown within conventions, accentuating the romantic element through song and dance that are meant to arouse desire, but at the same time sublimate eroticism.

Romance with a *tawaif* can last forever as long as marriage is avoided. Tragedy is inevitable if the *tawaif* tries to become a wife. In innumerable films of this genre, an ex-client recognizes her before or after marriage and hopes of a decent life are invariably crushed.

One of the classics of Indian cinema, *The Pure One* follows the usual pattern of the genre, confirming the power of social convention. When the priest asks the *tawaif* (Meena

Pakeezah / The Pure One (1971) by Kamal Amrohi, starring Meena Kumari as the melancholic object of fantasy

Kumari) her name at the wedding ceremony, performed on an open plateau, she does not answer. The groom answers for her and names her *Pakeezah* (the pure one). The distressed *tawaif* cries out 'Nahin!' and runs away, her black shawl flying out like the wings of an ominous bird. According to the Indian film critic Chidananda Das Gupta:

> It is a magnificent sequence enshrining the Turco-Arabic code of honour that requires total monogamous loyalty of the wife (if not ritual purity as in the case of the Hindus) to her husband (in Yılmaz Güney's *Yol*,

the family demands that the wife be killed by the husband for her sexual transgressions during his absence) . . . The effort to make a wife out of a *tawaif*, the film tells us, is doomed to failure.[3]

Such films have appealed to Hindus as well as Muslims, particularly in northern India. According to Das Gupta, the experience of the self that is divided between the wife and the *tawaif* revoked the lost Hindu tradition of the courtesan coming down from the mystical Urvashi to the Vasantsenas and Vasavadattas of the great classical cities of India.

Muslim filmmakers followed the status quo and showed the liaison with the *tawaif* within conventions rather than challenging the beliefs and prejudices of the audience. Some even heightened the existing biases by showing every action from the male point of view and blaming the woman for her unlucky fate. The fact that sexual tensions were not realistically pursued to fulfilment brought a sense of security to the family, which explains the popularity of the genre. Meena Kumari's *tawaif* was the most popular dancing girl of the city – her admirers ranged from the aristocratic Nawabs to the *nouveau riche* – but she still preserved her chastity. In fact, during the first encounter, the hero was allowed only a glimpse of her beautiful feet. When they were finally alone, he serenaded her with poetry, 'Let us go to the moon, beloved', not passion.

The Turkish version of Meena Kumari is Türkan Şoray, named *sultana* (a term once used to refer to the wives of

Ottoman sultans) by her public. Şoray created the myth of 'the woman to be worshipped'. She could remain a virgin even when she worked as a prostitute. She could live with a man for years without ever going to bed with him. Many women identified with her until the 1980s when the feminist movement began and an emancipated young generation emerged for whom these unbelievable stories decorated with false morality were at best a laughing matter.

Films about brothels and dancing girls had their heyday in Pakistan in the 1960s. Hassan Tariq extended the subject by adding orphans and illegitimate children. In the 1970s, he focused on glossy tear-jerkers about golden-hearted prostitutes who faced death for their sins such as in *Anjuman / Gathering* (1970) or *Umrao Jan Ada / Dancing Girl* (1972).

The genre was popular in Indonesia in the 1970s, introduced by Turino Junaedi with *Noda Tak Berampuan / Unforgivable Stain* and *Bernafas Dalam Lumpur / Panting in the Mud* (1970). As the titles suggest, the women in question have smeared their bodies with filth through their 'bad' behaviour, like their Turkish counterparts who are labelled as *kirletilmiş* (made dirty). Although they are not responsible for their misfortune, they must die to save society because sexually experienced single women are a threat to the integrity of men and the durability of marriage.

The highly predictable pattern of the traditional prostitute films is transnational: an innocent girl is betrayed by the man she loves or her honour is violated by the feudal village chief. Eventually she becomes a fallen woman. Despite occasional rays of hope (to be saved by the original lover or a kind-hearted customer), the tragic end is inevitable. Most of these films are concerned with the life of the woman after she has fallen and not the reasons behind the fall. The expediency of the subject matter in displaying female bodies while condemning them as polluted explains their immense popularity across cultures, particularly in closed societies.

At the opposite end from the prostitute, the bad woman, considered an urban malaise, is the good rural woman with an ill-begotten fate. Rural lives are more susceptible to the force of centuries-old traditions and religious dogmatism and, therefore, perfect material for stories about women's oppression and male dominance. *An-Nisa, Sura IV* (Women) – *ayet* (verse) *34* of the Koran appoints men in charge of women for the reason that Allah had made them superior. Good women are obedient. If they rebel, they have to be admonished, banished to beds apart and scourged until they obey.

Most rural women are unpaid workers in many countries even today, unable to achieve social or economical freedom. In traditional Islamic societies, they are sold to a much older man at a very young age and obliged to be wives and mothers in the house and workers in the fields. They are also entrusted with securing the continuation of the lineage, particularly important in the patriarchal system. Infertile women and those who cannot produce male heirs are forced to accept the arrival of a new wife.

Turkish rural melodramas present women as innocent, chaste, loyal and, most of all, silent creatures oppressed by all

Bataklı Damın Kızı, Aysel / The Girl From the Marshes (1934) by Muhsin Ertuğrul. Despite its pretentious approach to rural life, the film was very popular. The scarf Cahide Sonku wore in the role of Aysel is said to have started a folkloric fashion

male members of the family and exploited by the mother-in-law. Life in the village is shown as a constant struggle with blood feuds, oppressive landlords, equally oppressive customs and traditions, banditry, elopements and unrequited loves. Women are responsible for guarding the family honour. When this honour is lost, swarthy young village men become outlaws hiding in the mountains to plan their revenge and do not give up until they kill all the perpetrators, even if they have to sacrifice their own lives.

The first rural Turkish film was *Bataklı Damın Kızı, Aysel / The Girl from the Marches* (1934) by Muhsin Ertuğrul, adapted from Selma Lagerlöf's novel, *Töser fran Stormytorpet.* The protagonist, Aysel, is raped by the feudal landlord. When she gives birth to a child, the man accepts no responsibility. With the help of a kind villager, Aysel files a paternity and alimony suit against the aggressor.

The film set the precedent for stories of rape, pregnancy and abandonment, and Ertuğrul's voyeuristic presentations of some of the village customs found their niche in later years among imaginative filmmakers. 'Fountain eroticism', depicting young women at the fountain openly discussing men or flirting with them became very popular. Women washing the feet of their men coming from the field as a sign of respect was also a good subject for erotica, but it remained somewhat controversial as the act could also be interpreted as a manifestation of the slave status of women.

The rural woman of tears and suffering, the *ezik kadın* prototype, was created with *Boş Beşik / The Empty Cradle* (1952) by Baha Gelenbevi, a maternal melodrama about nomads with strong traditions and male-child fanaticism. In this film a young woman, oppressed by her family for seven years for her infertility, gives birth to a boy, but one day an eagle takes the baby who is sleeping in a cradle placed on the back of a camel. The mother reaches the nest of the eagle but does not find her baby.

The film uses the dilemma of infertility and love and the parallel baby–eagle–mother struggle within the context of colourful nomad life to enforce the tragedy. However, it fails to foreground the place and fate of women in a patriarchal society. It would have been too much ahead of its time, if it did.

Muhterem Nur, who played the young mother, fitted the role of the naïve and helpless village girl in her features and appearance. Her natural acting made her the star of similar 'emotional drainage' films. Over seventy schematic and superficial melodramas were made in the next decade, featuring Nur as the perpetually exploited village girl who loved her man, forgave him, ended up a 'fallen woman', but never rebelled. The titles of some of these films give a clear idea of their content: *Beni Mahfettiler / They Destroyed Me* (Talat Gözbak, 1951); *Piç and Zeynep'in Intikamı / The Bastard and the Revenge of Zeynep* (Memdüh Ün, 1958); *Ben Bir Günahsızım / I am Innocent* and *Kaderim Böyle İziş / This is My Destiny* (Nejat Saydam, 1960).

Like the prostitute films, rural melodramas lacked credibility. Made by urban middle-class casts and crews, without any serious study of the subject, with stars and starlets in folkloric costumes flushing their false eyelashes, such films displayed little semblance to the realities of village life. Their popularity lay in the fact that they represented models endorsed or rejected by the androcentric religious culture that relegated to the woman a secondary role, where the woman's silence and invisibility were the norms. For the producers, the profits from making the audience cry were more important than raising consciousness about the woman's oppression. (Similar subjects were to find meaningful interpretations in the hands of talented filmmakers, as in *Kuma* by Atıf Yılmaz and *Kaşık Düşmanı / Spoon Enemy* by Bilge Olgaç. See Chapter 4.)

With migration to the cities during a period of adjustment to Occidental capitalism, cinema diverted its focus to urbanization and the issues of migrant workers seeking an identity in a liminal space. The target was again oppressed and uneducated rural women, culturally outside the course of history or politics. Determined to invent a new identity for women who found themselves in a new society but still bound to old values,

Yeşilçam created submissive characters – faithful wives, devoted mothers and obedient daughters – who accepted suffering and humiliation arising from customs and traditions. Positive values were attributed to the lower classes whereas the upper class, particularly the more liberal urban population, was presented as corrupt. The conflict arose from the differences between the two and the message was usually transmitted through a lower-class woman.

'Lives were decorated with religious motifs and women were presented without sexuality – an orthodox point of view using certain patterns that still exist in Hollywood', Özgentürk explained to me.

These patterns were popular because rural women are conditioned to see pure love and a family formed according to the traditional laws of religion as ideal. Everything that is different from these laws (a different man, a different woman, a different law) has to be destroyed. In the tradition of Yeşilçam, just as in the Muslim religion, the woman has no place. She is someone who errs; who has to be physically punished when she errs. She is honourable only when she does not live. Her function is to remain an object for us to form the institution of family in the religious sense. If she cannot fulfil this function, her punishment is re-education by violence or confinement to 'sinful' spaces.

Turkish cinema from its beginnings endorsed conservative bourgeois values eschewing sexuality. Binarist constructions created one-dimensional, stereotypical characters that did not represent real women. Innocent girls never took off their clothes and never went to bed. To kiss, to undress and to make love was reserved for bad women – the vamps and prostitutes. To protect their careers, stars had to refuse bad woman roles. Films endorsed the sacrosanctity of marriage so as not to offend the family for whom cinema was the only entertainment before the arrival of television in 1968. Despite Kemal Atatürk's social reforms aimed at giving equal rights to women, taboos took longer to be broken, specifically concerning gender issues. Islam played a fundamental role in the patriarchal lifestyles of the rural population. Therefore producers took care not to insult the moral values of family women who constituted a large part of the audience. Cheap morning matinees for women were very popular, particularly with the star system of the 1960s.

Among various contradictions in Turkish commercial cinema is the figure of the *lumpen woman*, whose trademarks were the macho muscle power, the vulgar jests, mimicry, laugh, foul language and dress code of the male sub-culture. In the 1960s, when men were men and women were women, with nothing in between, the audience accepted such gender-benders that were in essence against the social, cultural and religious structure of the Muslim family, and the genre turned into a fetish. Metin Erksan's *Şöför Nebahat / Nebahat, The Driver* (1959–60) was so popular, sequels were made.

These women were expected to fight like men on screen, but act like women at home – to make love to men, be good wives in the kitchen and produce children. In a social structure that does not accept women as equal to men, such films distorted the women's predicament by creating schizophrenic characters and/or false images. They also confirmed the ingrained attitude that women could only be heroes if they acted like men.

The four top stars were typecast according to the so-called expectations of the audience. Türkan Şoray was the oppressed sexual woman; Hülya Koçyiğit, the oppressed asexual woman; Filiz Akın, the well-dressed little bourgeois woman, and Fatma Girik, the straightforward, honest, manly woman, known as *erkek Fatma,* male Fatma (which, incidentally did not mean to be unfeminine or masculine but only honest and brave 'like a man').

'Such roles were played as if wearing a mask similar to those employed in Oriental arts such as the *kabuki* theatre of Japan', Atıf Yılmaz told me during our discussion in İstanbul in 2003. 'The heroes could not become characters, as they did not have a psyche. When the medium of mass communication – television, video, internet – developed and borders with the world were lifted, whether they liked it or not, they had to become characters, able to come to terms with themselves and question their place in society.'

Müjde Ar, a younger and braver woman with a rebellious character, was the first actor to break the taboos by creating the image of an intelligent modern woman with sexuality. It took Türkan Şoray, the *sultana,* fifteen years to follow suit.

Pre-revolutionary Iranian cinema also had its fair share of *faheshe*, prostitute films. The 'deceived and deserted' woman who falls into bad ways was a popular subject, although the violation of her chastity was only depicted in a symbolic fashion. As in Turkey, women were often trusted with delivering the moral message of the film through stereo-typical dialogues.

During a period when a new wave of Iranian cinema promised a new vision of society and women, family melo-dramas such as *Tufan-e Zendegi / The Storm of Life* (1948) were made, drawing attention to the biases of the dominant patriarchal tradition. However, following the CIA-engineered coup d'état of 1953, the general cultural policies of the Shah led to the invasion of song and dance films with no cultural stimulus. Referred to by its critics as *film farsi*, the genre dili-gently copied the Indian commercial cinema that is today known as *Bollywood*. Provocative scenes were used abundantly, with or without narrative justification, to appeal to the fantasies of sexually deprived men. A plump and flabby dancer called Mahvash was the dominant sex symbol, so much so that in the provincial towns, screening of foreign films would often be stopped midway to present one of her dance numbers. After the premature death of Mahvash, other dancers followed and cinema continued to treat women as sex objects.

During the 1960s, films targeting the single young men of the lower middle classes and banking on their suppressed sexual drives showed women as gullible, weak creatures, destined to become prostitutes or cabaret dancers, unless saved by a good-looking muscular man. These cheap fantasies had nothing to do with the real women (or men) of Iranian society, but no one seemed to mind.

Amid such masculinist approaches, there were a number of noteworthy works such as *Khesht va Ayeneh / The Brick and the Mirror* (1965) by Ebrahim Golestan. Still focusing on a prostitute, the film tried to look beyond the surface into the dreams and hopes of 'fallen women'. The commercial cinema, however, continued to regard women as sex objects, designating them degrading roles as cheap belly dancers, prostitutes, maids or weak creatures who could easily be raped by any man. A look at some of the titles from the Seventies should give a clear idea as to the nature of the films: *Yek Chamadan Seks / A Suitcase of Sex; Showhar-e Pastorizeh / Pasteurized Husband; Ruspi / Prostitute; Zan-e Bakereh / The Virgin; Defa' Az Namuus / Chastity Defended; Dokhtar Nagu, Bala Begu / Calamity Girl.*[4]

At the end of the 1960s, Masud Kimia'i's second film *Gheysar* (1969) heralded the arrival of the New Wave of Iranian cinema, which brought a new vision that proved to be equally damaging to women. These avant-garde films not only pushed women to the margins, but also created a distorted image by blaming them for all social evils. *Gheysar* endorsed the values of a male-dominated Islamic society in a story of rape, murder and revenge setting the precedence for several vengeance stories that showed helpless young girls who could not defend their chastity by themselves, forcing their menfolk to butcher everyone to reclaim the lost honour of the family. Sex and nudity were added to inflate the market.

The reforms of the 1960s and 1970s gave certain political rights to women without giving them social and personal rights; women remained the private property of men. A woman could become a minister, but could not travel abroad without her husband's permission. She was constantly under the control of the State and the family. Cinema ignored the increasing number of women who entered the workforce, politics or educational spheres, or depicted the image of this 'new woman' as corrupt and immoral.

Bahram Beyza'i is perhaps the first Iranian filmmaker to present realistic women characters on screen with his first feature, *Ragbar / The Downpour* (1972). Unprecedented in Iranian cinema, his *Garibeh va Meh / The Stranger and the Fog* (1974) placed the woman character in an important position. Beyza'i continued to make films about the lives of Iranian women, but they were forbidden after the revolution because they showed women in close-ups and without the *hejab*. He made one of the most beautiful films of Iranian cinema in 1985, *Bashu, Gharibehye Kuchak / Bashu, the Little Stranger*, about an unusual relationship between a woman with extraordinary communicative powers and a boy orphaned during the Iran–Iraq war.

In Pakistan, family melodramas and romantic love triangles were the fashion until the late 1970s and the military regime of General Zia-ul Haq. When his government took absolute control of the media in a campaign to Islamize the country, the film industry received an irreparable blow. The censors were strict on sex and nudity but quite liberal on violence. Violent Punjabi films became very popular, creating a 'brave man' genre about a Robin Hood hero (Sultan Rahi) who fought corruption. The middle class that had once patronized cinema was alienated by the rise of these macho films, which presented women only as seducers with loose morals.

In the 1980s actor Shamim Ara, crowned as the queen of big budget Urdu films with music, sex and outdoor romance, became a director and producer. She created a female version of the avenging hero *(Lady Commando)* that was just as violent as the Sultan Rahi characters. Love stories with exotic (foreign) outdoor locations became very popular in the 1990s. These films displayed the female body regardless of the narrative, borrowing Bollywood's wet sari formula or presenting risqué scenes (for instance, scenes involving teenage girls) as dreams to avoid censorship. The song and dance numbers that relied heavily on gyrations of the pelvis left nothing to the imagination. Ara even produced a series of 'Miss' films – *Miss Hong Kong, Miss Colombo, Miss Singapore, Miss Istanbul* – without ever dwelling on women's issues.

In Bangladesh the social realist tradition of Bengali cinema was prevalent in the 1960s, with a focus on the lives of semi-urban people and the loyalty of women in contemporary settings. Following the war of liberation in 1971, formula melodramas with clichéd morals began to invade the screens. According to film historians the murder of Sheikh Mujibur Rahman, the founder figure of Bangladesh, in 1975 and the subsequent political events that pushed the country to right-wing reactionarism and Islamic conservatism had their repercussions on the film industry. Several films were made with Arabic titles, carrying Islamic messages. At the same time, to launder black money, shady businessmen were producing cheap sex fare with ample violence and a very sexist approach to women. Serious cinema was totally pushed to the margins.[5]

Interestingly, the situation is very similar to the Turkish experience of around the same time. In a period of political instability, when the government tried its best to curb the creative talent of committed filmmakers such as Güney, Turkish screens were also inundated with soft-porn films, stimulating the rise of an alternative way, the Islamist cinema. In both cases, the result was the alienation of middle-class audiences, for long enthusiastic patrons of cinema.

Central Asia, which was under the yoke of the Soviet regime for over seventy years, boasts a centuries-old tradition of strong women characters. During the Soviet period, however, equality of the sexes was determined by the Communist Party and adapted to the economic and social needs of the country, and cinema reflected these policies. For instance, the cliché of 'suffering mother' was very popular in 1950s Kazakh cinema. The archetype of the Central Asian woman was a self-sacrificing creature devoted to her family and children, an image that is the basis of the Muslim understanding of woman, according to film critic Dilyara Tasbulatova, who maintains that

> A Moslem, even if he is officially atheist, is a highly orthodox creature. He can be a 'rocker', an academi-

cian or speak three European languages – it does not essentially change anything. At least not for women. It is precisely this quality – this insuperable orthodoxy – that does not allow him to look at his surroundings with a sober eye. Instead, a certain self-satisfaction . . . colours his view. It acquires a tone of elevated romanticism, an almost ingratiating sweetness. All of this, essentially, points to absolute indifference. A Moslem is always indifferent to women . . . So why should he not be indifferent to his representation of them? This, perhaps, explains the dominance of the stilted, stereotypical female characters, which flood our screens.[6]

Despite such a pessimistic outlook about the representations of women, conscientious filmmakers with earnest socio–political concerns have existed transnationally. Lütfi Akad's *Vurun Kahpeye / Hit the Whore* (1948), adapted from a novel by Halide Edip Adıvar, is one of the early examples of serious Turkish cinema with a positive woman protagonist. Set during the war of independence, the film focuses on the struggles of a progressive teacher against fundamentalism in a small Anatolian village. Aliye represents the idealist enlightened woman of the Kemalist generation; she is patriotic but also feminine, ready to die for her country and for the man she loves. Unfortunately, she falls victim to the conspiracies of the fanatic local *imam,* who provokes the villagers to lynch her for treason. The film is important for exposing the evils of backwardness and

Vurun Kahpeye / Hit the Whore
(1948) by Lütfi Akad

religious fundamentalism rampant in post-independence Turkey. Islamist extremists stopped the projection in many areas of Anatolia although the film was never officially censored.

In the 1960s, following the 27 May 1960 coup d'état, rural films gained a veristic dimension. The inspiration was the upsurge of realistic novels of the soil, initiated by talented writers such as Yaşar Kemal. Metin Erksan's *Susuz Yaz / Dry Summer*, a film in the socialist realist genre, exposed men's obsession to possess (the land, the water or someone else's wife) receiving the Golden Bear at the Berlin Film Festival in 1964, the only Turkish film ever to win this award. Erksan, who has always maintained a personal style, is considered the first *auteur* of Turkish cinema.

Yılmaz Güney created a reputation as the macho man of commercial cinema with his roles in countless male bravura films. He was the *çirkin kıral* (the ugly king) of Yeşilçam. Several years after his premature death in exile, it is still argued whether the macho image is the underlying point of view in the films he scripted, directed and/or produced, despite the international accolades that these films have brought. *Seyyit Han* (1968) displays in a realistic fashion the fate of the rural woman who sacrifices her happiness for the honour of her family. Seyyit Han (played by Güney in Clint Eastwood style) is a brave loner who is in love with Keje from the next village but before he can have her, he has to deal with his enemies. Keje's brother does not want his sister to be a widow. After seven years and long jail sentences, when everyone assumes him dead, Seyyit returns to claim his bride just as she is about to wed the village headman, Hamdi Bey. Keje is ready to run away with Seyyit but when her brother reminds her that the honour of the family is in her hands, she sends Seyyit away. As the men dance and shoot their rifles into the air to celebrate the wedding, Hamdi Bey makes insidious plans to mend his hurt pride. He buries Keje's body in the ground and covers her head with a basket, challenging Seyyit to a marksmanship contest. Seyyit falls into the trap and kills the woman he loves.

The film foregrounds the silence that contaminates women's lives in feudal societies regulated by strict codes of behaviour. The 114 *sura* of the Koran (which incidentally are all addressed to men) define the borders of the relationship of

Seyyit Han (1968) by Yılmaz Güney, an experiment in crossing genres (folkloric, romantic, fantastic, neo-realistic and supernatural) featuring Güney as the brave loner doomed to kill the woman he loves

women with men and the superior position of men rather than establishing the rights of women. *Al-Baqarah, Sura II – ayet* (verse) *223* informs men that their women are their field to cultivate, meaning the woman is the man's collateral. He can love her or abuse her. The laws of religion and morals are on his side. Keje accepts being buried alive to save the family honour. Like many other Anatolian women, her fate is decided by her brother, her husband or the village head.

Sürü / The Herd (1978) by
Zeki Ökten

Sürü / The Herd (1978), Güney's collaboration with Zeki Ökten, carries the motif of the silent woman in the character of Berivan, who stops speaking after losing her third baby. Berivan is given in marriage to Sivan from the rival clan to end the long feud that has killed many. Although the couple love each other, happiness and peace are denied to them by the patriarch father-in-law who accuses Berivan of draining their lineage. Sivan tries to defend his wife, reminding his father that as his wife, Berivan represents the honour of their family, but his father believes that love for a woman makes a man weak. Sivan's hopes of finding a better life in the city and a cure for Berivan's illness collapse when the sheep they were suppose to sell in Ankara perish on the long train journey. Berivan dies alone in the corner of a construction site.

The focus of the film is the disintegration of nomad life and the patriarchal structure with changes in the economic structure. Women seem to be at a double disadvantage when placed in liminal spaces although feudal oppression is presented as a force destroying men and women alike. Sivan, a grown man, is unable to raise his hand against his father when the latter beats him like a child. Subsequently, he beats his wife for refusing to speak.

Women and honour is the main theme of *Yol / The Way* (1982), written by Yılmaz Güney and directed by Şerif Gören. One of the masterpieces of Turkish cinema, the film draws attention to the unchanging destiny of the rural woman: she is born a slave and dies a slave. While Seyit Ali is in jail, his wife Zine is accused of smearing the family honour. Men of her clan lock her inside the barn and wait for the husband to come and execute the punishment, which is no less than death according to customs and religion. *An-Nisa, Sura IV – ayet* (verse) *15* of the Koran requires men to call four male witnesses if their women are guilty of indecent behaviour. If the witnesses testify to the truth of the allegation, then the woman should be confined to the house until death takes her or until Allah shows her a way.

Zine has no choice but accept the fate chosen for her by her clan. Her father (a blind old man who is still the dominant patriarch) warns Seyit Ali: 'For eight months, she is tied with a chain like a dog. For eight months, she did not see the light of day. It is *haram (forbidden)* for her. For eight months, not a drop of water touched her body. This is what she deserves . . . *Şeytan* (Satan)! She thinks she will evoke your pity. Don't let your heart soften, don't let your hand tremble; wipe this mud off our face; don't you ever pity her.'

Seyit Ali's heart is burning with revenge, but he does not have the courage to execute the deed himself. Instead, he creates the conditions (forcing her to cross the snowy mountains where another woman has just frozen to death) for Allah to punish her. He is a victim of a society that enforces on individuals feudal customs; his cowardice will haunt him all his life and yet he cannot disobey.

Women are shown as accepting the traditions imposed by men unconditionally. Zine's sister-in-law shows her pity as a woman who has erred, but she will not accept the gold coin Zine offers her because it was acquired by selling her body. There is

Yol / The Way
by Şerif Gören
from a script by
Yılmaz Güney
(1982)

no doubt in her mind as to the justification of the punishment. She tells Zine that her destiny is in the hands of her husband, she will live if he wants her to live and if he doesn't . . .

Boys also grow up believing what the family head tells them. When Seyit Ali informs his son that they will be going to his uncle's place, the boy does not want to take his mother along: 'She is dirtied', he says.

Although the Seyit Ali episode is at the core of the narrative, the film also follows the stories of four other prisoners on leave, each one in a problematic situation with a woman. Mevlut cannot be alone with his fiancée. When the couple take a tour in the bazaar, two women in black chadors, designated by her extremely conservative father as chaperones, follow them. When they go into a *baklava* (sweet) shop, the two chaperones sit at the next table. During the few moments that they have together, Mevlut becomes a macho man:

Mevlut: When we get married, my word will be the law in the house. For instance, if I say black, you will know that it is black even if you think that I may be wrong. You will accept it and not answer back. As my wife, you will not talk much, to talk to men and joke with them is a definite no. I would get angry, very angry. Apart from your brothers and relatives, you are not allowed to talk to anyone's man. You won't do anything against my word. You won't wear what you want. I will decide what you wear, what you do. OK? *(Meral listens to all this with admiration, often shakes her head in approval, laughs.)*

Meral: OK. You speak so nicely. Did you learn all of this in prison? [7]

Mevlut goes to a *meyhane* (a bar frequented by men) to get drunk. 'I don't understand all this, which century are we living in?' he asks the brothers of the girl. 'This is our custom, our tradition, what is there to be angry about? Don't you know the people's tongues?' is the answer. To vent his anger, he enters a brothel. On the wall of the room where he has sex with a prostitute, among the rules and regulations, the price, caution to use condom, etc., we see written, 'God's word is the deed', a common Muslim expression.

The third prisoner is Memed, who cannot rejoin his wife Emine and their children because he is held responsible for the death of Emine's brother. Emine's love for her husband overcomes her sense of filial obligation and she runs away with him. On the train, they lock themselves in the toilet to quench the natural thirst of their bodies but nothing escapes the all-watching eyes of the crowd that is about to lynch them, screaming 'Immoral microbes! Infidels!' While in police custody, they are murdered by Emine's youngest brother who is determined to cleanse the family honour.

Ömer, a Kurdish man who leaves jail with no intention to return, falls in love with a girl he sees only from a distance. Although his feelings are reciprocated, he must marry the widow of his murdered brother as the custom dictates. No one bothers to ask the opinion of the widow. As for the young girl, the only way she can speak is with her eyes. The fifth prisoner, Yusuf, never makes it to his village. For lack of proper papers he is taken into custody at the beginning of the journey.

Unlike traditional Turkish rural melodramas that structure the narrative around the highest-ranking male member of the family, usually the father who maintains the patriarchal ideology, the films of Güney show the collapse of such a system. *Seyit Han*'s protagonist is a loner without a family. The father in *The Herd* is like a raging bull, still with enough authority to oppress those in a lower rank in the family hierarchy (his son, his wife, his daughter-in-law), but helpless against the changes in society that render his position obsolete. In *Yol*, Zine's father, who endorses her death sentence, is shown as a blind old man with one foot in the grave.

Roy Armes, in his seminal work *Third World Filmmaking and the West*, assesses Güney's attitude toward women as puritanical, pointing to the fact that the role of women is inevitably seen as subservient to men. 'Throughout his work, women are stolen and abused, seduced and abandoned, sold, killed, or driven to suicide. To have a woman – as wife or daughter – is to be vulnerable: she will be killed or will betray you, and in either case the called-for response will be violent revenge – the vendetta that runs as an undercurrent through society in all Güney's work.' [8]

Several Turkish filmmakers I have interviewed support a similar point of view, declaring Güney's cinema as 'macho'. Ali Özgentürk, who knew Güney as a friend, master and colleague has a different opinion:

> Violence in Güney's cinema is the violence inherent in society, in man–woman relations and in existence. In societies like ours, love is not like the trembling of a branch in the wind. Our world carries the essence and rhythm of violence. Yılmaz (Güney) was a man of this society, not a modernized, domesticated, assimilated man but one that expressed himself with his gun, his manhood and his cinema. His cinema is not different than the way he lived his life or the way he treated women. If he loved a woman, to kill himself for her or to kill her was natural behaviour for him. You may call it 'macho'. What would you think of a man who falls onto the grave of the woman he loves in *Seyyit Han*?

For Yılmaz Güney the question was not a struggle between men and women. During several interviews he conducted after receiving the coveted Palme d'Or at the Cannes Film Festival for *Yol,* he stated that it was impossible to talk about Turkey without talking about women. 'A society where women are not free cannot be free', he has stated on many occasions.

> When I show the oppression of women, I also show the humiliation of men. Mevlud's short moments with his fiancée are chaperoned by two women in black chador; Memed's longing for his wife shames him in front of society; his brother-in-law becomes a murderer at a tender age to save the family honour; and Seyit must kill his disloyal wife as religious customs dictate. Ömer's decision to join the mountain guerrillas could be a courageous act, but still he is a coward, just like Seyit Ali, for obeying traditions and letting down the woman he loves. State oppression and the residues of feudalism that safeguard patriarchal Islamic traditions have turned life into prison for all citizens.[9]

In that sense, what Pierre Bourdieu says about manliness and honour in Muslim Mediterranean societies in his seminal work, *Masculine Domination,* sums up the message of Güney in the three films discussed above:

Gelin / The Bride by
Lütfi Akad (1973)

If women, subjected to a labour of socialization which tends to diminish and deny them, learn the negative virtues of self-denial, resignation and silence, men are also prisoners, and insidiously victims, of the dominant representation. Male privilege is also a trap, and it has its negative side in the permanent tension and contention, sometimes verging on the absurd, imposed on every man by the duty to assert his manliness in all circumstances. Inasmuch as its real subject is a collective – the lineage or the house – itself shaped by the demands which inevitably remains, in many cases, inaccessible. *Manliness*, understood as sexual or social reproductive capacity, but also as the capacity to fight and to exercise violence (especially in acts of revenge), is first and foremost a *duty*.[10]

In the 1970s, agriculture lost its dynamism when the Turkish government gave priority to industrial development and migration to the cities intensified. At the outset, the new environment did not change the dynamics inside the family. Women were still expected to exist under male authority, not to work outside but to give support at home. Most films of this period of spatial activity do not question the male authority and if they do, they do it superficially.

The Anatolia trilogy of Lütffi Akad, *Düğün / The Wedding* (1974), *Gelin / The Bride* (1973) and *Diyet / Blood Money* (1975), is very important in manifesting a realistic approach to the effects of social changes on the lives of rural people, especially women. All three films are attempts at a realistic narrative displaying the customs and traditions of each family. At the centre is the woman as Mother, the backbone of the family. Each film alludes to a religious motif that serves as the essential trope. *The Bride,* the most successful film of the trilogy, is the story of a family that has just settled in Istanbul. Although they are not poor, the family structure, lifestyle and mentality display deeply rooted feudal and patriarchal values. The motivation of the uprooted men is to make money as fast as they can. Meryem's fight against the family to take her sick son to a doctor proves fruitless and the boy dies, symbolically on the day of the *Kurban Bayramı,* the religious holiday when devout Muslims sacrifice sheep. Determined to take her destiny in her own hands, Meryem leaves home to work in the factory. Her husband does not kill her as tradition demands, but joins her to begin a new life.

The title of the film is significant. The word *gelin* meaning 'the bride' or 'the daughter-in-law' has a pejorative meaning: within the feudal system, she is the most exploited one, without recourse to rebellion. Akad's Meryem, however, is not a weeping willow. She represents the new woman that migration to the city has created; she is in a position to play a role in her fate and, at the same time, to be a binding force for the family with her maternal characteristics.

In the 1980s more women joined the work force and their new experiences posed a challenge to the traditional family values disrupting the patriarchal order. For some women, economic independence was an open door to escape male oppression and to take control of their own lives. However, the appearance of the working woman did not automatically free cinema from the status quo. Yeşilçam continued to present work outside home as acceptable only under economic conditions. Under the masculinist conventions, women could not be shown in administrative positions. They were expected to *serve* society as teachers, nurses, bank clerks, secretaries or housemaids. When they earned money, they brought it to their husbands or brothers to restore the strained male ego. It took a long time for commercial cinema to accept that the silent and submissive motif failed to present a true picture of women's multiple statuses and the dynamism and creativity of their activities.

Şerif Gören gave noteworthy examples of the 'independent woman' with *Derman* (1983), *Kurbağalar / The Frogs* (1985) and *Firar / The Escape* (1986) and the motif soon became one of the most dealt topics. In the following years, with the feminist movement at its height and so many recently liberated women sharing the work force at all levels, films focusing on the fantasies of women who have repressed their desires in the past, due to the extreme conservatism of Muslim society, gained importance. Sexual relations began to be depicted in a more realistic fashion.

The most important aspect of these new films was the way they fragmented the family that had been the norm for commercial cinema since its beginning. The Turkish cinema of the 1980s either ignored the family or narrated its disintegration. Women were no longer the founding stone of the family, bearing the burden of keeping it together, but independent beings trying to find solutions to personal problems. The works of Atıf Yılmaz (discussed in Chapter 5) are good examples of this new trend.

Where the trend failed was in regard to more affluent women. Although women's magazines lost no time changing their target from the family woman to the career woman, cinema marginalized them by creating characters whose sexual behaviour drastically deviated from the established norms. Women filmmakers fell into the same trap, and showed women in powerful positions relegating this power, without much fight, to the men they loved and becoming slaves to uncontrollable male desires. The focus of these films was not the career of the woman, but her achievements regarding the opposite sex. Such an attitude created a problem of identification for women audiences.

Career women appeared in other Muslim cinemas around the same time. In Iran, Dariush Mehrjui presented a woman architect in *Ejareh neshinha / The Lodgers* (1986) and a painter/designer in *Hamoon* (1990). The latter focused on the psychological problems of women arising from oppression imposed by tradition, a theme that Mehrjui has developed further in his later work (see Chapter 4).

In Pakistan, Hassan Askari created a self-supporting independent woman journalist in *Doorian / Distances* (1984). The sensitive rendition of her fight for the custody of her son after she separates from her rich and influential husband won the film many national awards.

Although genuine working woman characters are rather rare in popular Indonesian cinema, a new image of a woman disrupting the patriarchal order was created in the 1980s as the *rebel woman*. However, Krishna Sen points out in her book, *Indonesian Cinema*, that under the strict censorship laws of the country, this new image was not a representation of women, but a metaphor for forbidden controversial topics including race, religion and class conflicts. Since the regime was not concerned with gender politics, films could conveniently use women characters to express critical opinion, inadvertently opening new possibilities for their representation.

A good example of a *rebel woman* film is *Roro Mendut* (1984) by Ami Priyono, inspired by a well-known legend. The eponymous female hero is captured and given to ageing General Wiroguno by the king as a gift during the coastal expansion of the central Javanese kingdom of Mataram in the seventeenth century. When she refuses to give in, heavy taxes are imposed on her as coercion. She uses her sexual charms to make money selling half-smoked cigarettes from behind a screen, seducing men by the silhouette of her full lips. When she falls in love with Pronocitro and tries to elope with him, the general kills the boy in a sword fight and Mendut kills herself with the general's dagger.

At the beginning of the film, Mendut's resistance symbolizes the regional struggle of Java's coastal periphery against the Central Javanese heartland. When she falls in love with a man she can no longer be safely used as a symbol, without her also representing the woman in control of her emotions and sexuality. Since such a woman presents a danger to society, her suicide is the only solution. According to Sen:

> Mendut's successful rebellion is only doomed when she allows her own passions to be aroused, rather than using her sexuality to arouse men. In the patriarchal symbolic structure there is no space for an unattached sexual woman. In the last scene, instead of seeing the aging General through Mendut's eyes, the camera presents her from his perspective . . . this reciprocity of looks, in terms of Mendut's look defining the men and their looks defining her, disappears from the moment Mendut looks at and desires Pronocitro. It is her initiative that sets up their first meeting, which is the turning point in the camera's positioning of Mendut. From this point on, both the look and the action belong to the men.[11]

Apart from the *rebel woman* films, which relied on political *double entendre*, women have maintained their traditional subsidiary roles in many genres of Indonesian cinema. From historical films, comedies and thrillers to martial arts, commercial cinema has continued to focus on men's world. The sentimental genre that concerns itself with relationships within the traditional family structure – a working father, housewife mother and school-age children – is perhaps the only arena for women to appear as visible characters in commercial cinema.

In the 1990s, with the extraordinary advances in communications, rapid globalization and the rise of fundamentalism, new situations were created all over the world. Despite common misconceptions, women have made remarkable gains in Iran, although the fight for individual freedom is still far from won. New Iranian cinema (discussed in Chapter 5) reflects in a realistic fashion women's present place in that country.

In Central Asia, cinema, along with other aspects of society, also had to be recreated after independence. In Uzbekistan, where traditions and religion play a strong role, Yusuf Razikov, a prominent filmmaker entered the film industry making light comedies to reflect on social, moral and psychological issues. His first film, *Voiz / Orator* (1999), is a gentle satire on the battle of the sexes, layered with subtle nuances about totalitarian regimes.

Just before the Bolshevik revolution of 1917, Iskander lives happily with his three wives, which is permitted by the Islamic law of *sharia*. Faithful to the teachings of the Koran, he devotes equal love and care to all three and everyone is happy. However, Communism sees man and woman as equal and does not sanction polygamy. He begins to give propaganda speeches to enable him to continue his blissful life, but his skill in oratory attracts an emancipated commissar who falls in love with him and tries to disperse his wives.

Razikov's next film, *Ayollar Saltanati / Shenskoje Zarstvo / Women's Paradise* (2000) is also a comedy about the battle of the sexes, at least on the surface. Olim, the artist is suffering from writer's block and having difficulties organizing his relationships with several free-spirited women. The big question that faces him is whether to love one woman who stands for all women, or to love all women. His long quest for an elusive young woman turns into a surreal dream journey that lands him at a women's market with all the women of his life – a false paradise, so to speak. Razikov explained to me that these women serve as a metaphor for Olim's art and his inability to be successful in his art. The hero is in crisis at both emotional and creative levels.

Both films are important achievements for Uzbek cinema. Whereas *Voiz* is a subtle commentary on life during the Soviet regime, *Ayollar Saltanati* is a discourse on the relationship of the artist to his art. In terms of gender issues, however, a masculinist approach prevails. Women are portrayed as level-headed but, at the same time, as 'sweet trouble' for men. Man–woman relations are framed within their traditional boundaries: man as the artist, woman as the muse; women seeking marriage and stability, men searching for new experiences; middle-aged man with no particular sex appeal apart from the unwritten law of the superiority of his

The Last Stop by
Serik Aprimov (1989)

gender seducing a beautiful young woman. Both films show men at their happiest when they can have several women. In both films, women accept these conditions as natural and resort to devious methods to survive rather than trying to bring changes.

Kazakh critic Tasbulatova maintains that times have changed for the worse for Central Asian women. Strong women characters whose humour, beauty and intelligence were an inspiration to storytellers for centuries are not to be found in today's novels or films. For her, the present-day screenwriters satisfy the demands of realism using clichés, which are, ironically, taken from the Koran.

She considers Serik Aprimov, one of the important representatives of the Kazakh New Wave that had its golden period in the early 1990s, an exceptional filmmaker in approaching women characters.

> I still have not seen the self-aware, full-blooded, vital women who appear in *Last Stop* in a single other Kazakh film. Men have a tendency to go to extremes, they see women either as saints or as whores. But Serik's women fit in neither category . . . he loves his heroines, in spite of everything . . . To love a licentious young village woman who casually sleeps with the protagonist from time to time; to love an old woman who quietly puts up with her son's drinking bouts; to love the quiet girl who had been virtually in bed with her lover when his friends came around, and then primly refuses to drink with them; this is all understandable. But Serik also loves the fat woman who killed her illegitimate baby to hide her 'sin'. His love is not the condescending love of a righteous man towards a sinner. There is neither sexuality, nor philanthropy in his love. Simply, he understands this woman.[12]

Turkish cinema, which has gained a new vitality in recent years after a long period of low productivity, seems to relegate women and their concerns in favour of a more global outlook. Filmmakers I have spoken to agreed on the contention that Turkish cinema is still a 'macho' cinema that endorses the status quo. Well-developed women characters are still rare. 'When trying to focus on women, cinema still employs clichés', according to Özgentürk.

> Filmmakers, both male and female, display the man's point of view. The old cinema used the good woman–bad woman clichés; the new cinema uses the clichés of feminism in the name of modernism. The structure of Turkish society is a schizophrenic one, always in extremes and out of tune with the values of nature. Double standards dominate men–women relations. Many issues that have been resolved in the West have just arrived here and create problems. Unlike literature, where several good women writers have created plausible characters, our cinema does not reflect the position of real women, which is much ahead of cinema, or rather in an altogether different place.

Zeki Demirkubuz is perhaps the only one among the new generation of filmmakers who creates living women characters. He draws his inspiration from the traditional Yeşilçam cinema that he experienced first-hand during his long years of apprenticeship, but with skilful neologism creates personal stories that are also very political. His films uncode, decode and deconstruct the customary clichés of Yeşilçam and

Üçüncü Sayfa / The Third Page by Zeki Demirkubuz (1999). As a new arrival to the big city, Meryem is caught between tradition and modernity

deliver a fatal blow to the status quo, its trademark.

Demirkubuz's women are not idealistic or theoretical constructs but individuals with their own problems and feelings, and are very much part of the time and space they occupy. In *Üçüncü Sayfa / The Third Page* (1999), loosely based on Dostoevsky's *Crime and Punishment*, İsa and Meryem (the names are Turkish transcriptions of Jesus and Mary) are two marginals who live in a dilapidated apartment building in the back streets of downtown Istanbul, the big metropolis. Meryem is a pretty peasant woman trying to survive in a male-dominated society. She is subject to violence and harassment by her alcoholic husband and by the dubious landlord, both turned on by the pornographic movies they watch on the satellite channels. Naturally, she trusts no one.

Extricated from her roots, she is confined to a basement flat where her only connection to the outside world is the TV screen. In her liminal state, the soap operas she watches day and night shape all her actions and reactions. Often it is not evident whether she is able to see the difference between real life and make believe.

Meryem is a woman caught between tradition and modernity. She comes to the aid of İsa to pay his debt to the thugs who harass him, but she is taken aback when they ask for dollars; she is not yet versed in the new economy. What she knows is that survival means exploiting others. Her character has had its precedent in the hero of Atıf Yılmaz's *How Can Asiye be Saved?*, who also finds salvation in doing to others what has been done to her.

The film's closed form (most action takes place in small rooms or dark hallways) creates a claustrophobic atmosphere. The only outdoor scene is in the children's park at night, where the darkness is foreboding. Meryem's movement towards more open spaces leads her to a false paradise, symbolized by a large apartment on the upper floor and possessions to match those she had envied on the TV screen. Her *yemeni* (peasant scarf) that covered her long hair is gone, displaying a bouffant hair-do copied from the TV screen. From her point of view, she has arrived, the cost is not important.

Masumiyet / Innocence (1997) is a road movie with a minimalist story about marginal characters. The film presents two very different women: Uğur is a prostitute who lives with her pimp and her deaf-mute daughter and moves from town to town, singing in cheap bars. Hardened by years of exploitation, she is an aggressive woman, accustomed to unorthodox ways of survival. The second woman is the sister of the male protagonist, Yusuf, who had killed her lover, aborting their elopement and sending her back to her resentful husband.

She is the 'silent' woman as she has destroyed her tongue by shooting into her mouth after the incident. Yusuf, recently out of jail, oscillates between these two women. His sister is a typical poor family woman whose honour has to be protected, whereas Uğur is from a world that considers women merchandise. Both live in worlds dominated by men. The difference is that Uğur's 'fall' is her liberation, whereas the sister's 'honour' is a curse. Uğur's reckless life, following from town to town the man she truly loves (who is constantly shifted from one prison to another), brings her closer to death each moment, but at least she chooses the life she lives. Yusuf's mute sister does not have this chance.

Demirkubuz questions traditional moral values in a provocative fashion, drawing attention to their variability in lower cultures. A woman who is judged as a 'fallen woman' by society can also be conceived as someone with individuality who merits respect, while another woman can be punished with violence for her 'innocent' love. Yusuf is the personification of the double standards of Muslim men. He does not hesitate to kill his sister's lover to clean his family honour, but is willing to pimp for a prostitute (and even marry her if she accepts him).

If the women of Demirkubuz are untrustworthy, scheming two-timers who only look after their own interests, this should not be taken as a manifestation of misogyny on the part of the filmmaker. Rather than hatred, Demirkubuz displays empathy for the type of woman created by Turkish society. Meryem of *The Third Page* knows how to take care of herself because no one else will do so. No matter which way

Sri by Marselli Sumarno (1998)

she turns, she will receive a blow. Her husband is useless, her lover is worse. Would another man be different? Everyone is pushed to the corner and of course will hit back, as she argues. Kindness does not pay for Meryem of *The Third Page* or for Uğur of *Masumiyet*. They are products of a new society that has destroyed human values.

The protagonist of Indonesian Marselli Sumarno's first feature, *Sri* (1998) is not much different from the characters of Demirkubuz. She also is a survivor in a male world, although her methods are less unconventional. The film is set in decadent Solo where men gamble and womanize. The eponymous hero, a young peasant girl, marries a 70-year-old Javanese aristocrat named Hendro to improve her social status. When

Hendro falls sick, as a loyal wife, Sri tries to nurse him back to health, but after his death, she emerges as an independent woman and takes over his business. Sumarno explained to me that the title, *Sri*, has three meanings in Indonesia: the prefix for addressing royalty, a common name for women, and the rice goddess that represents life and prosperity.

> All these symbols form the identity of an unassuming, restrained but at the same time power-conscious version of a modern Javanese woman. She is able to continue her daily routine of selling batiks as she watches her husband slowly die. 'I have my own dreams', she says to him. 'If you live, I share them with you but if you die, I pursue my dreams.' She tries everything to keep her husband alive. As a last chance, she tries to make a pact with Yamadipati, the God of Death, to dance with her. However, the time has come and the husband must die. And when he dies, she sits on her husband's chair with resignation but in graceful silence.

In the new millennium, with wars in Afghanistan and Iraq further disrupting the shaky balance of the region, Pakistan and Bangladesh have seen an upsurge of violence by Islamist fundamentalists targeting cinemas. Theatres have been bombed and videos burnt in public squares recalling similar attacks during the Islamic revolution in Iran, which claimed hundreds of lives. It is remarkable that, even under such circumstances, bold filmmakers do not shy away from exposing atrocities

Lalsalu / A Tree Without Roots
by Tanvir Mokammel (2001)

committed in the name of religion, particularly against women.

Tanvir Mokammel, an important voice of Bangladeshi cinema, explores faith and deception in rural Bangladesh, where a totally subjective *fatwa* from a *mulla* can bring down a death sentence on innocent victims, mostly women. *Lalsalu / A Tree Without Roots* (2001) focuses on a religious charlatan who wilfully misinterprets the ideals of Islam and exploits the villagers for his gains. He is a real patriarch to his first wife who obeys him unconditionally as a God-fearing wife. In the denouement it is revealed how much he actually is dependent on this silent woman. The film is based on a novel published in 1948, but still very relevant to rural life in Bangladesh.

Khamosh Pani / Silent Waters (2003), a Pakistani film

Khamosh Pani / Silent Waters by Sabiha Sumar (2003)

made mostly with European money, is focused on religious intolerance. Sabiha Sumar has previously made several documentaries on the plight of women in her country. *Silent Waters* takes place in 1979 during the regime of Zia, at the height of fundamentalism. However, the film is not about religious intolerance in one specific time or place, or injustices committed by one specific religion against the other. What is certain is that in times of strife, women are easy targets for aggression.

Atrocities of the partition of India in 1947, when Sikhs as well as Muslims abducted and/or raped the women of the other faith, are shown in flashbacks. Many families force their daughters to suicide or push them down wells to save the family honour. The protagonist Veero, a Sikh woman, refuses to jump into the well as demanded by her father and, like several others, later marries her abductor, accepting his faith and changing her name to Ayesha. Now a widow, she gives Koran lessons to support herself and her son Salim, an intelligent but misguided young man, a good candidate for Zia's men to recruit to the cause of Islam. When the government authorizes pilgrimage to the Sikh shrine in the village, many pilgrims arrive from India. One of them is Ayesha's brother. Anger and fear at the discovery of his mother's secret pushes Salim further into the arms of the fundamentalists and he leads the violent campaign against the pilgrims to force them to leave the village.

The film presents Veero/Ayesha not as a victim, but as an individual who is able to come to terms with her life. Even her final suicide is not an act of weakness but rather a protest against all forms of intolerance. The abduction scenes, which are shown in sepia, out of focus, flashback, are far from voyeuristic. Unlike countless commercial films that exploit violence against women for the sake of sensationalism, the main thrust of the film is the life of the victim after the incident rather than the incident itself. Despite certain weaknesses in terms of the development of some of the supporting characters, Sumar's first feature is significant in drawing attention to religious intolerance and particularly, violence against women in times of conflict.

2 violence against women and the politics of rape

Violence threatens the lives of women both inside and outside the family, and in developing countries as well as developed. In addition to conjugal violence, women are often subject to rape motivated by revenge, as in Pakistan, given death sentences by *mullahs*, as in Bangladesh, or murdered by male relatives for smearing the family honour, by acts at times as simple as going to the cinema, as in south-eastern Turkey. Young girls are victims of trafficking in Indonesia, sold for less than the price of a goat. Such violations are often considered 'normal' as the woman is someone else's wife, someone else's maid or someone else's daughter and, therefore, private property, according to sexual terrorism reports. As for violence within the family, *An-Nisa, Sura IV– ayet* (verse) *34* of the Koran ascribes to men dominance over, but also responsibility for, the women under their care, which gives them licence for abuse as well as respect. According to Bourdieu:

> Like honour – or shame, its reverse side, which we know, in contrast to guilt, is felt *before others* – manli-

ness must be validated by other men, in its reality as actual or potential violence, and certified by recognition of membership of the group of 'real men' . . . Practices such as some gang rapes – a degraded variant of the group visit to the brothel, so common in the memoirs of bourgeois adolescents – are designed to challenge those under test to prove before others their virility in its violent reality, in other words stripped of all the devirilizing tenderness and gentleness of love, and they dramatically demonstrate the heteronomy of all affirmations of virility, their dependence on the judgement of the male group . . . What is called 'courage' is thus often rooted in a kind of cowardice: one has only to think of all the situations in which, to make men kill, torture or rape, the will to dominate, exploit or oppress has relied on the 'manly' fear of being excluded from the world of 'men' without weakness . . . Manliness, it can be seen, is an eminently *relational* notion, constructed in front of and for other men and against femininity, in a kind of *fear* of the female, firstly in oneself.[1]

The repeated portrayal of women as the sources and recipients of male anger and frustration, and the linking of violence and sex in people's minds, have been food for cinema since its inception. Although some films use violence against women as a metaphor, often the woman herself is the victim. In some films, rape appears as an instrument of indirect political oppression of men, who are linked through an unequal power relationship with the rapist. In others, the woman is used as a scapegoat in an revenge situation between rival groups. The fact that most rapes end in the suicide of the victim is an indirect warning that there is no recourse for a woman who cannot protect her honour.

Cinematic interpretations of violence against women are often exploitative in nature, using scenes of rape as a licence for exhibitions of sexual acts or nudity. Rape scenes objectify women through carefully choreographed shots, sound effects, lighting and props. According to Das Gupta, whenever rape is made attractive, the male audience is being asked to gather vicarious satisfaction.

> It is analogous to the cry of 'kill him, kill him' at boxing matches. No revenge device, however inventive, can wipe out the subtext of sexual satisfaction left between the lines of this moralistic tale. In our films, rape alone can provide the opening for the frank and open sexuality that is sublimated by the song in love stories in difference to the squeamishness of the audience and its protectors. Only the rapist, that is, the criminal, is allowed an open expression of the animal in us. It is safe to watch him at the act, because he stands condemned already as an outsider to decent society. If you get a secret, vicarious satisfaction from watching the act, there is no need to talk about it. The chorus of disapproval will drown such talk anyway.[2]

Turkish culture defines the rapist as *namus* or *ırz düşmanı* (enemy of honour), but violations of 'honour' are often exploited for erotic purposes by commercial cinema, particularly in rural melodramas. In film after film, the feudal landlord or his son lusts after an innocent girl, kidnaps and rapes her. After the incident, the brave village boy who has been harbouring a secret crush on the girl hides in the mountains to prepare his revenge. On his return, he kills everyone who violated his beloved, to save her honour. Some rural films show graphic gang rape scenes, such as *Koçero* (1964) by Ümit Utku, in which villagers violently attack city girls.

In urban films, bourgeois women, who are considered too liberal to care about their honour, are the most common targets of rape. In *İffet / Honour*, Kartal Tibet proves himself to be on the side of violence, showing the chauffeur lover of a bourgeois woman push her head through the rear window of the car and close the window. While her head is stuck in the window, he rapes her from behind. (The film was a box office hit. Many went more than once to see this scene.)

Rape and violence against women gain a new dimension in the hands of Metin Erksan, who presents the sexual impulse as a subliminal force. The protagonists of his films are possessed by their obsessions in a psychopathologic way.

Erksan's most controversial film, *Kuyu / The Well* (1968), considered as one of the classics of Turkish cinema, is a rural drama that focuses on a relationship, founded on male obsession and female resistance, which culminates in tragedy.

Kuyu / The Well by Metin Erksan (1968). 'Be my wife or I'll kill you.'

Based on a newspaper article, but decorated with the fantasies of Erksan, the film displays the helplessness of an oppressed but level-headed young village woman against the perverse determination of a man obsessed with her.

The film opens with Osman watching Fatma bathing in the river, the classic narrative convention that generally forewarns the audience of imminent sexual violence. Osman steals Fatma's clothes and, pointing a gun to her face, delivers an ultimatum: 'Be my wife or I'll kill you.' When she resists, he ties a rope around her waist and pulls her through the arid landscape to coerce her, but she does not want to give herself to a man she does not love. When she escapes, runs after her, grabs her and pushes her to the river. 'Water cleanses all sins', he says. As she lies down on the grass in silent defiance, the camera views Osman from her perspective telling her that the woman is created from the tiny little bone of the man and that is not without reason. There is a reason behind everything God does. He did that for the woman to walk behind her man. Women should always obey men!

Osman is arrested, and Fatma returns to the village where men gossip about her. On his release from jail, Osman again points a gun at Fatma's face and rapes her (the scene is not shown). She escapes again. Osman is arrested once more. Fatma's mother finds her a husband, a middle-aged fat man called Ibrahim. After all, not many men want to marry a girl kidnapped twice.

There is a long shot of Fatma on horseback as a bride, but then she runs away. The groom blames the mother, using an old proverb: 'One who does not beat her daughter beats her knee.' Another man declares that 'the meat that the dog smelled should not be eaten'. The mother blames her black destiny. As Fatma is getting ready to hang herself, Mehmet, a fugitive from death row, saves her. The camera distances itself as the two lie on a rock in the sun. The rural police kill Mehmet, and Fatma returns to the village still wearing her bridal headgear. Her mother kicks her out for disgracing the family and she finds a job serving in a cheap bar. Osman comes out of jail and kidnaps her a third time. He tells her he is determined to marry her even if she is a whore. She says he made her a whore and she'll never say 'yes'. He ties her up again and the same desperate journey begins.

When Osman climbs into a well to wash his face, Fatma throws stones at him. In a dramatic shot, her head is framed within the circle of the mouth of the well with the light behind, while he is groping in the dark below. Fatma's patience culminates in revenge, albeit with violence, after which she has no choice but to kill herself.

The Well is structured around the obsession of a man, but the woman is not a passive character. Within her limitations she stages a resistance. Perhaps she is not able to win a physical battle against the brute force of her aggressor, but she succeeds in wounding him at his Achilles' heel, his manhood. For someone like him to be refused by a woman, a creature of the lower species, is tantamount to losing his manhood, which must be restored at all costs. That is why he kidnaps her repeatedly. At the end, his death by water is a kind of relief. Water cleanses all sins.

For a large part of the film, Fatma is literally tied to Osman with a rope and dragged up and down the slopes, but Erksan's master narrative saves this motif from becoming monotonous or even ridiculous. The rope becomes a symbol of men's sovereignty over women for centuries, especially in the rural milieu, the paradisiacal landscape of arid mountains and gushing rivers alluding to the Garden of Eden. The woman, who constantly tries to cut this rope, is freed only when the man dies and then she cannot stand living alone. (In *40m² of Germany* by Tevfik Başer, a village girl is practically held prisoner by her brute husband in a tiny German flat, but when she is finally liberated by his death, she does not know what to do or where to go. The confusion of Fereshteh, in *Two Women* (see Chapter 4), after the death of her tyrannous husband is similar.)

From an artistic point of view, the film is one of the masterpieces of Turkish cinema. The minimalist narrative works in repetitions; the characters of the two protagonists who are both loners in an indifferent world are developed meticulously and with special concern for human psychology; societal dynamics are sharp; and the characters that are offsprings of such a society very accurately drawn. The photography and the camera angles are beyond reproach. However, the film's graphic display of male brute power is controversial. While many consider *Kuyu* as an important representative of the cinema of resistance and argue that Erksan has brought a special sensitivity to the situation of women in Turkey, the feminists condemn it as the sexual fantasies of a macho man. Erksan claims that the film takes its inspiration from the message in *An-Nisa, Sura IV – ayet* (verse) *19* of the Koran, which states that it is not lawful for men to possess women by force. They should consort with them in kindness because if they hate them, they hate a thing wherein Allah has placed much good.

Sexual violence against women at times serves as a symbol for the political and social impotence of men in a system that systematically strips them of power: they do to women what the state does to them. In Central Asian cinema, for instance, there has been a strong tradition of using women as a metaphor for the state and its distorted values. Lynne

Attwood points out that with the arrival of perestroika, anger towards the Soviet State began to be expressed on film by violence against women.[3] However, this is not the only reason for depictions of violence against women in films. Often the woman herself is the victim, not just a symbol.

Films made in the 1960s in Pakistan have a strong tendency to show violent death as the only fate awaiting women. In Khalil Qaiser's *Shaheed / Martyr* (1962) about British imperialism in the Middle East, the Arab heroine sets herself on fire and jumps into an oil well to become a martyr. In S. Suleman's *Baji / Sister* (1963), the young widow who falls in love with the hero lies dead in the downpour on the eve of his marriage to a younger woman. Saroor Barabankavi's *Akhri Station / Last Station* (1965), shot in Dhaka, shows the protagonist as a crazy woman with a cigarette, in a small railway station, who is brutally raped on the platform and eventually crushed by the train. In Khursheed Anwar's *Humraz / Confidant* (1967), one of the two identical twin sisters is imprisoned in a deserted mansion, tortured and finally declared insane so that her estate can be grabbed. In the director's previous film, *Ghunghat / Veil* (1962), the woman character is already dead but reappears as a ghost to win back her husband. In Raza Mir's *Lakhon Mein Eik / Unique* (1967) a Hindu girl who is raised in Pakistan returns to India, but is not accepted by a conservative society and dies while crossing the border. One wonders what kind of women would watch the films that display overtly sadistic tendencies towards women, physically and/or psychologically.

Chitra Nadir Pare / Quiet Flows the River Chitra by Tanvir Mokammel (1999)

On a more artistic level, Nazrul Islam's *Khawhish / Bitter Truth* (1993) draws attention to the indifference of society and the justice system to violence against women through the story of a gang rape and vengeance story. Pakistani actress-producer Saima Pirzada's *Inteha / The End* (1999) takes up the pressing issues of wife-beating and marital rape, which is often concealed not to bring 'shame' to families. Her brave approach won her several National Awards.

Tanvir Mokammel from Bangladesh is another conscientious filmmaker who depicts human atrocities and violence against women, particularly, with a humanistic approach. *Chitra Nadir Pare / Quiet Flows the River Chitra*

(1999) focuses on the persecution of a Hindu family during the partition of India in 1947. Believing East Bengal to be the common inheritance of Hindus and Muslims who have fought for the Bengali language and cultural identity, the family of eccentric lawyer Shashikanta Sengupta refuses to move to India. Their children grow up playing with the Muslim children. However, during the 1964 riot between the Hindus and the Muslims, Basanti, the widowed daughter of Shashikanta's brother, who lives on the other side of the river, is raped. Basanti commits suicide by drowning herself in the Chitra. The film depicts individual sadness in the backdrop of larger-than-life events. Mokammel uses the rape of Basanti to foreground the prevalent sense of violence, not to add a sensationalist aspect to the film. The act itself is visualized through suggestive cinematography. Basanti's subsequent suicide, however, ratifies the dominant contention that only death awaits women who are no longer pure.

Bernafas dalam Lumpur / Panting in Mud (1970) by Turino Junaedi is considered the first Indonesian film to feature a sex and rape theme with explicit and vulgar dialogue in the tragic story of a village woman whose search for her errant husband leads to her eventual fall. The film was a commercial hit although banned in several provinces.

According to Karl G. Heider, Indonesian cinema has had a long history of presenting sexuality as sadism.[4] Good examples are the Japanese Period films that show Japanese soldiers raping Indonesian women in visually explicit scenes. *Kompeni* films, dealing with the Dutch colonial period, also show Dutch soldiers raping village girls. Ironically, when the narrative involves love or tenderness, the sexual aspect moves off-screen.

The horror genre presents graphic sexuality in a sadistic manner. Distasteful misogynist films such as *Snake Queen* (1982) by Sisworo Gautama Putraad and its sequel, *Hungry Snake Queen* (1986), have tried to capitalize on the popularity of the Hong Kong horror genre and have appealed to a certain audience. Although these films do not show real nudity, scenes of the hero eating the breasts of women are not uncommon.

Perumpuan, isteri dan Jalang / Woman, Wife, Whore (1993), Malaysian U-Wei bin Hajisaari's first feature, is a daring film in the context of Malaysian culture. The protag-onist is a free-spirited young woman made powerless by the patriarchal society. Then she discovers where her true power lies, her sex. To reach such awareness and sense of freedom, she has to come to a point where she has nothing to lose.

On the day of her marriage to Amy, Zale-Haa, a sweet village girl, runs away with another man. Amy chases the lovers all the way to Thailand and kills the man. To humiliate Zale-Haa he sells her to a pimp for three dollars over a period of six months. At the termination of the contract, he returns to claim his woman with the intention of displaying her in her village as a prostitute. On the way they are stopped by the vice squad and Amy is obliged to marry Zale-Haa to save his skin. Back in her natal village, Zale-Haa is badly treated by Amy and left alone for long periods. She causes a social upheaval by sexually provoking men and encouraging women to liberate themselves from social conventions. Soon she begins to make friends and her 'bad influence' grows. Women forego their traditional *sarongs* and dress like her, in provocative city clothes; they answer back to their husbands; young girls become dissolute. Amy, who goes from village to village selling vegetables, becomes very angry when he hears the rumours about his wife's sexual activities. He returns to the village for revenge. In the final scene, all the adults of the village gather at the square, looking relieved at the death of Zale-Haa. Children play, oblivious to the tragedy. Order has been restored.

The film won several National Awards when it was shown in Malaysia after 36 cuts and the removal of the word *whore* from the title. Women's groups attacked U-Wei for displaying prolific violence against the protagonist and for creating a hero whose resistance to such violence is minimal. His answer to such criticism, when I met him in during the Festival of 3 Continents in Nantes, was that some women were against the film because he portrayed the dark side of Malay women, and that those who protested were 'sexually repressed'.

U-Wei revokes the association of sex with guilt in creating a free-spirited protagonist who is flesh and blood and far from stereotypical. In essence, the film is an indictment of the double standards of traditional societies that suppress individuality. Zale-Haa's murder carries the elements of ancient ritual sacrifices. However, one wonders if even the best intentions should justify such violence on screen.

3 islamist cinema as a genre

A cinema with a strong religious ideology and morals started in secular Turkey in the 1970s when migration from the country to the city gained impetus. *Milli Sinema* (National Cinema), as it was called, had evolved as a reaction to the trashy films of the commercial cinema and the socially and politically committed films of the left. While the latter were fighting against long-established commercial rules to create a more realistic, original and contemporary cinema, with Yılmaz Güney leading the way, a small group around Yücel Çakmaklı tried to win back the alienated conservative and traditional audience with so called 'nationalist' stories. These stories were built within the framework of commercial considerations, but always with a religious message. (*Milli Sinema* was in fact Islamist cinema, but it could not openly be advertised as such as item 163 of the constitution forbade using religion for such purposes.)

In the 1960s, hastily made 'Prophet films' depicting the lives of the prophets had been popular, particularly in certain regions of Anatolia. The first 'Islamist' feature film, *Birleşen*

Yollar / Crossing Roads was made in 1971 by Yücel Çakmaklı. Although its commercial success was largely due to its star, Türkan Şoray, *Birleşen Yollar* became the prototype for Islamic films that used the same formula of a love interest between an innocent traditional person and a degenerate modern one. These stories generally ended with the discovery of the true path by the modern person; sometimes this was too late for a happy ending. The clash of the good and old with the bad and new served as a vehicle to expose the theme of the suffering of Muslims under an unjust and non-Islamic system.[1]

It is ironic that the year 1990, which saw the veil of censorship lifted over Yılmaz Güney's *Umut / Hope* (1970), was also the year Yücel Çakmaklı brought to the screen *Minyeli Abdullah / Abdullah of Minye,* narrating the sufferings of a man dedicated to Islam. The box-office success (530,000 viewers) of this film led the way for a new upsurge of religious films.

In a symposium organized by the Islamic Fund in the early 1990s, fundamentalist 'intellectuals' vowed to 'Islamize' the newspapers, cinema, TV and the theatre, calling on industrialists who had been building mosques to invest in the arts. With art began the alienation of people from their roots, they claimed, with art it will be thrown out. As every movement needs a name, Islamist journalist Abdurrahman Sen called this new zeal for religious propaganda on screen *beyaz sinema* (*white cinema*). The first Istanbul *white cinema days* were held in October 1991.

The audience for this kind of cinema was generally Anatolian with rural roots but now living in an urban environ-

Umut / Hope, poetic realism by Yılmaz Güney (1970)

ment. The melodramatic and sentimental content and the tear-jerking, soap-opera style attracted women more than men.

Money for these projects came from the Gulf countries, German guest workers and devout business people, although *white cinema* as a genre remained specifically Turkish and did not have any transnational links with parallel movements elsewhere. However, several filmmakers tried to raise the issue of a transnational Muslim brotherhood, exploiting international conflicts in which Muslims seemed to be the targeted victims, such as Bosnia and Chechnya.

Mesut Uçakan's *Yalnız Değilsiniz / You Are Not Alone* (1990), a film with blatant religious propaganda, appeared in a period when Islamist political parties were gaining ground and became very popular, especially among young women. The film focuses on the tribulations facing those who choose a devout life style. Serpil, a modern girl (presented wearing a mini-skirt and riding a bicycle) feels alienated from her family due to the decadent lifestyle of her parents, who drink, play

left: Yalnız Değilsiniz / You Are Not Alone by Mesut Uçakan (1990)

below: Mesut Uçakan, Islamist filmmaker from Turkey

poker and flirt with the opposite sex. Influenced by her religious grandmother, she decides to embrace Islam, replacing her mini-skirt with the long overcoat and headscarf that is the identifying outfit (*tesettür*) of devout Turkish women. Her parents attack her for disgracing their reputation; her classmates feel sorry for her. Even her 'feminist' cousin (dressed as androgynous *chic*) does not take her seriously. The film ends when she is forced to check into a clinic for a probable psychological disorder. The sequel to *You Are Not Alone* began with the release of Serpil from the clinic and focused on the issue of *turban* (the headscarf) in the universities and the government's attempts at blocking headscarf-wearing women from entering the examination rooms.

Mesut Uçakan presents the struggles of these women as a Human Rights issue. During an interview in Istanbul, he told me that the secularization of Turkey with the establishment of the Turkish Republic in 1923 has created an identity crisis, alienating people from their roots. The hybridized youth has turned to the West in a vacuum created by the misinterpretations of history.

The position of the supporters of *white cinema* as regards the history of Turkish cinema is very similar to that of Ayatollah Khomeini and his followers as regards pre-revolutionary Iranian cinema. One Islamist producer claims that since the foundation of the Turkish Republic, with few exceptions, cinema has served negative aims instead of directing society, and particularly youth, to positive channels. Masses who lacked the necessary education were influenced by the negative images that were presented on screen and people became alien to their own beliefs and cultures. There is a certain amount of self-criticism, as well blaming the conservative faction for ignoring cultural and artistic activities for so many years instead of exploring their possibilities.

One of the essential criticisms of *white cinema* against the mainstream was the depiction of women. They maintained that the outlook of the mainstream cinema on women was similar to that of *cahiliyye*, pre-Islamic Arabia. (According to the Koran, during *cahiliyye* women were the lowest elements of society, even below animals.) Mainstream cinema presented women as commodity or sex objects, they argued. However, neither *milli cinema* nor its offshoot *white cinema*

Yalnız Değilsiniz II
/ You Are Not Alone II
by Mesut Uçakan
(1991)

showed any sign of involvement with the problem of women. In *Abdullah of Minye* women are shadowy figures, seen but not heard. *You Are Not Alone* presents cardboard characters: feminist women look butch and emotionally unstable; undevout women cheat on their husbands; young university students spend their time at parties, taking drugs and flirting with the opposite sex. Even those women who crusade for their right to wear a headscarf are so unbelievable that one wonders how the film expects to send a moral message to the audience with their sermons.

The sequels to *You Are Not Alone* and Çakmaklı's *Abdullah of Minye* relied on the success of the earlier films and did not receive the same interest. Several projects were halted because actors refused to play in such films, afraid of being labelled reactionaries. Producers blamed the secular media for marginalizing religious cinema, but *white cinema* received criticism even within the sector, several Islamist magazines declaring the films not worthy to be called a work of cinema.

Film historian Nijat Özön maintains that it was perhaps because these films 'tried to bring a solution to the complex problems and value judgements of a rapidly changing society with fossilized religious and moral understandings' that they have remained marginal.[2]

Muslim socials, which reached the height of their popularity in the 1960s in India, are very similar to *white cinema* films in the way they propagate Muslim values, particularly regarding relations between men and women. However, they are very different in two grounds. First, unlike *white cinema* with a political agenda to discredit the dominant secular ideology, *Muslim socials* are apolitical. Second, they maintain a certain cinematic standard and can be watched with pleasure even by non-Muslim audiences. This is in sharp contrast to *white cinema*, which is of poor artistic quality and of no interest to the majority of audiences.

The dominant *Radha-Krishna* tradition in India emphasizes the present and the desire to capture the moment with joyful love. The *Laila-Majnu* tradition of Muslim culture, on the other hand, sees love as the essential desire of God and regards earthly love as a preparation for heavenly love. The absolute devotion of the woman to the man, marital fidelity and loving secretly but without guilt are important aspects of this tradition.

Mehboob Khan is credited with the best contemporary *Muslim social*. *Najma* (1943) became such a big hit that it remained a prototype of *Muslim socials* for 40 years. A number of girls born around 1943 were named Najma after the virtuous heroine of the film. *Elan* (1947), a film about good education and the bringing up of children, was considered as one of the best *Muslim socials* of the period.

Mere Mehboob / My Sweet Love (1963) by H. S. Rawail is the most popular *Muslim social* to date. A romance set in Lucknow, supposedly at the beginning of the twentieth century, the film's moral lessons are so embedded in the sweet love story and song and dance numbers that for the audience they are like sugar-coated pills. Anwar, an aspiring poet, bumps into veiled Husna on campus and falls madly in love with her after a single glimpse. He composes a love song and wins the Urdu literature award after singing it at the college concert. Whether it is meant to describe earthly love or heavenly devotion, as it is supposed to, the poem is quite explicit:

> *I will caress you with my eyes*
> *Envelop me with your fragrant tresses*
> *Console me with your gaze*
> *Lift your veil . . .*

Subsequent meetings of the lovers are disturbed by unfortunate coincidences. Husna's brother Nawab Sahib, who is like a father to her, turns out to be the benefactor of Anwar's sister, Najma, who is like a mother to him. The problem is that she is a fallen woman. Innocent and pure at heart, she has sacrificed her life singing and dancing for men, so that she could educate her brother to become a doctor like their father. Nawab Sahib is a liberal minded man who does not mind marrying his sister to a penniless poet like Anwar, but he has no intention of marrying a woman with a shady past. He has a lesson or two to learn about life, but at the end what is not supposed to happen, does not happen.

The long-lasting affection between Nawab Sahib and Najma is presented as asexual. 'Brother, I swear on the Holy Koran, our love is pure', Najma assures Anwar. Classical lines from the film endorse family values such as 'A child's paradise lies at the feet of his mother', 'Love is worthless compared with the honour of your parents' or 'I know duty is a heavier burden than love.'

The film never questions ingrained patriarchal values, but rather endorses them. Nawar Sahib cannot marry Najma because his honourable family has remained 'unsullied' for centuries. 'How can I make a bride of a face people see as stigma and scars?' is his rhetorical question. Najma can only ask for forgiveness and assure him that she had never had such dreams. 'It is not necessary for love to wear wedding clothes, my lord.' Although she trusts him in every respect, it does not take long for him to suspect her motives when his family interest is in question. All she can do is beg forgiveness for the sins she did not commit.

Everyone is good in the film; everyone is sacrificing something; everyone wants to die for honour. No one bears a grudge against anyone for anything.

Muslim socials slowly faded away with the arrival of television, changes in social structures and, according to some in the industry, with the rise of Hindu nationalism.

In January 1979, during his famous speech at the Behesht-e Zahra cemetery, Ayatollah Khomeini stated that the Revolution was not opposed to cinema, only obscenity. Pre-revolutionary cinema, which catered to Occidental colonialism, alienated the youth from their roots. It had to be denounced to fight corruption. During the ensuing fervour, more than 180 movie theatres were burned by fanatic arsonists. The revolutionary guards arrested many filmmakers and actors, confiscated their possessions and banned the screening of their films. Several film personalities were indicted on charges such as corrupting the public and were purged. Others went into exile. About 2,200 previously shown domestic and foreign films were re-inspected, only around 200 receiving screening permits. Film production entirely stopped.

The period immediately after the revolution, now referred to as the First Republic, began with the creation of the Islamic State. Ayatollah Khomeini and his radical followers gained control over reformist and modernist factions and established *Feqh*-based Islam. The Committee for Cultural Revolution was created to control culture and arts and the Ministry of Culture and Art became the Ministry of Culture and Islamic Guidance (MCIG), with the purpose of Islamizing all arts and cultural activities.

Before the revolution, cinema was among the forms of art declared *haram* by the clerics. For devout Muslims, going to the cinema was equal to committing a sin. According to Ziba Mir-Hosseini, the main reason behind such denunciation was that cinematic representations of women and love upset the delicate dualism which had long attended these topics in Iranian culture. Love has always been the main theme in Persian poetry, but it is seldom clear whether the writer is talking about divine or earthly love, or (given the absence of grammatical gender in Persian) whether the 'beloved' is male or female. Both the Persian language and the poetic form have allowed writers to maintain and even work with these ambiguities. The art of ambiguity (*iham*), perfected in the work of classical poets such as Hafez, has spoken to generations of Iranians . . . But such ambiguity cannot be sustained in the performative and graphic arts, where both the language and the form demand greater transparency and directness in the depiction of women and love. Among the traditional solutions adopted for this problem were the complete elimination of women, as in *ta'ziyeh*, the religious passion plays, where women's roles have always been played by men, or idealized and unrealistic representations, such as the 'neuter' figures depicted in paintings of the early Qajar period, which were embodiments of how the 'beloved' was described in classical poetry. By the late nineteenth century, with the advent of photography, the representation of women had become more realistic. The drive for 'modernization' under Reza Shah, and the corresponding take off of cinema as public entertainment in Iran, reinforced this tendency. Not only had Iranian women's public roles and status changed, but women and love stories were integral to the film industry from the start.[3]

Islamic authorities were aware of cinema's relevance for reconstruction and re-education. However, *feqh* did not have any clear guidelines about cinema, apart from labelling images and themes as *halal* (permissible) or *haram* (forbidden). The First Republic promoted the creation of a distinctively Islamic cinema for the purposes of spreading religious guidance. A new set of highly restrictive censorship codes were formulated, which brought film production under the tight control of the government.

Focus was on traditional moral values; these were delivered through didactic slogans inserted into the dialogue. *The Scarecrow* (1984) (a prizewinner at the 1st Fajr Film Festival and a very popular film for a long time) purveyed the message that stepmothers were not always evil; *Seeking Refuge* advocated control of one's ego, which would lead one to salvation, and *Nightbreaker* warned about the evils that can come with addiction. These themes were repeated with each film. The dominant message was it was never too late to turn over a new leaf. The regulations also dictated that the films had to have a happy ending. Even today, many films culminate in a happy ending with or without narrative justification (see Chapter 5, *Taraneh*).

Censorship's main concern was the representation of female characters. The clerics have interpreted the Koran personifying women as dependent nonentities who could never play major independent roles. To show a woman in a story or a play could only arouse passion and lead men astray. To allow women to sing or dance in public was out of the question. It was best to keep them *sangin o somet* (solemn and silent). If they had to appear at all, they had to be shown as modest and chaste characters whose *raison d'être* was to be obedient wives and dutiful mothers. Depiction of love on screen was the biggest challenge to filmmakers since the laws forbade physical contact between opposite sexes. Even a mother sending her son off to war could not touch him while saying goodbye. Films that tried to give the feeling of intimacy through the eyes were bowdlerized by the religious censors who declared only one kind of look as *halal*, the sisterly look, with the condition that it had to be a long shot.

Strict rules of censorship created confusion for filmmakers. To maintain the universal cinematic standards expected by their audience while exercising auto-censorship became the biggest challenge. One outcome was the elimination of women characters all together. For example, *Telesm / The Spell* by Dariush Farhang (1986) is about a powerful princess who disappeared in the hall of mirrors of her castle. This way, the woman protagonist does not have to appear on screen. (In the 1990s, Iran's highly esteemed woman filmmaker, Rakhshan Bani-Etemad reversed the trend and eliminated the male character from the screen in *The May Lady* by constructing a partially epistolary love affair. See Chapter 4.)

As women and love were absent from the screen, emotions were channelled through children, and stories with child protagonists dominated the screens. Several established filmmakers of today (Abbas Kiarostami, Majid Majidi, Jafar Panahi, Abdolfazl Jalili) began their careers making films with child heroes.

Towards the end of the First Republic, increasing numbers of artists and intellectuals raised opposition to the restrictions. *Feqh*-based Islam made it almost impossible for art to present a holistic picture of society. The Farabi Cinema Foundation was established in 1983, as the executive branch of the cinema department of the Ministry of Culture and Islamic Guidance with its motto 'Supervision, Guidance, Support'. Their productive assistance and the gradual loosening of *feqh*-based ideology resulted in the production of quality films that began to attract international audiences.

When Mohammad Khatami became the Minister of Islamic Guidance and Culture, he declared that cinema was not the mosque, which gave a certain amount of hope to the industry. However, he had to resign under pressure in 1992. He was elected president in 1997 with strong support from the film community and has been re-elected for a second term. Several projects waiting for approval for many years (such as *Do Zan / Two Women* by Tahmineh Milani) have received the green light in his presidency.

Notions of public and private are very clear in Muslim societies. *Hejab*, the Islamic code of dress women are obliged to support in public, was endorsed in cinema following the Revolution and still carries its force regardless of the relaxation of the regulations over the years. The Ministry of Culture's little red book published in the summer of 1996 confirms the strong hold of *hejab*. In 1998, the newly appointed Minister of Culture and Islamic Guidance, Dr Ataollah Mohajerani repeated the requirements for Iranian films to receive a screening permit: 'The issue of *hejab* is an accepted norm in our society and cinema industry. In other words, no filmmaker should expect to show a woman without a scarf, even when she is in her kitchen preparing food for her husband. In tune with jurisprudential and religious decrees, men and women are not allowed to touch each other, even in a simple handshake. This is a decree, and we cannot overlook it.' [4]

Resourceful filmmakers have been stretching their imaginations to create works with semblance to reality. In *Gabbeh* (1996), Makhmalbaf avoided violating a ban on showing a woman giving birth on screen by donning a skirt and playing the role himself. He shot *Nowbat-e Asheqi / Time of Love* in Turkey. The authorities told him love did not exist in Iran, as he explained to me during an interview. *Sokut / Silence* was shot in Tajikistan because in Iran he could not show a young girl dancing. Several established filmmakers, such as Majid Majidi and Abdolfazl Jalili, continue to shoot rural scenes where the rules of *hejab* are not so strict.

Abbas Kiarostami used men and children in his films until *Ten* (2002). The protagonist of *Ten* is a modern young woman of means driving a 4-wheel-drive in the mind-boggling traffic of Tehran. She is buckled up in the confines of her car as many women have been tied to their home. She only carries women except for her young son, who alone represents the world of man. The outside belongs to men.

Sokut / Silence by Mohsen Makhmalbaf (1998) was shot in Tajikistan

Inside the car is a world without men, but men are the main subject of conversation. Women leave the car to buy an anniversary cake for them, to make a request at their tomb or to solicit them. The boy reproaches his mother for divorcing his father and pursuing an independent lifestyle. Despite the fact that she is professional and autonomous, she is expected to stay at home, tied to the kitchen, to preserve the ideal form of family as endorsed by masculinist societies. To divorce a husband she no longer loves, she has to resort to devious means such as accusing him of being a drug-addict or wife-beater. Incompatibility or lack of love is not a valid reason. Apart from various tropes that are quite evident, the film can be considered an allegory of Islamist society and cinema. Both try to relegate women to identities constructed by religious ideology or its dogmatic interpretations, undermining the evolution of women in a world constantly in motion.

4 women's films, films about women

Tahmineh Milani is a militant feminist filmmaker from Iran, committed to voicing women's issues through the medium of the wide screen. She cautioned students during her speech at the University of Tehran in December 1999 that there was an urgent need for a women's cinema. She stresses the fact that she did not mean merely hiring more women in the film industry – having more women directors, writers, camera operators or actors. What was important was not the gender of the filmmaker, but making films that reflected women's perspectives and experiences. She did not think that current films tried to discover or display what Iranian women in today's society were thinking.

Her sentiment is shared by Rakhshan Bani-Etemad, one of the leading filmmakers of Iran. Bani-Etemad told me during an interview that before the revolution, women were depicted either as prostitutes or as 'trouble' for men. After the revolution, filmmakers fell into another trap. To meet the expectations of the society, model characters such as good mothers were invented, creating a myth. Rather than depict-

Rakhshan Bani-Etemad

ing women as human beings with positive and negative attributes, filmmakers formulated icons that were very far from real women. She admitted that before *Banoo-e Ordibehesht / The May Lady* (1998), she also created characters she would have liked to see and not real ones.

Bani-Etemad is one of those courageous women who decided to stand behind the camera to have their voices heard. Like several others of her gender, who were working non-professionally in the industry, she was fired after the revolution. With her creativity and determination, she used the new situation to launch a career as a director and started making socially committed documentaries. Later she used her research material to create fictional heroes that are realistic portraits of the women of her country.

In contrast to the pre-revolution period that had very few women working as filmmakers, several are actively involved in the industry today and their works have been inter-

Nargess by Rakhshan Bani-Etemad (1992), an Iranian *ménage à trois*

nationally recognized. Young Samira Makhmalbaf's accomplishments are a good example. However, only two, Rakhshan Bani-Etemad and Tahmineh Milani, of different temperament and approaches, consistently address the issues of women in their films.

Bani-Etemad pushes the cinematographic limits of her country by focusing on taboo subjects such as poverty, crime, prostitution, polygamy, divorce, repressed feelings, illicit love and similar realities of social existence. The women in her films, be they factory workers, thieves or filmmakers, are individuals who question their personal identity and their place in society. Her films place gender relations in their cultural and political perspective in a period of transition from a traditional Islamic society to modernity and question the andro-centric mores that have regulated women's lives for centuries.

Her first three features, *Karezhj Az Mahdudeh / Off the Limits* (1988), *Zard-e Ghanari / Yellow Canary* (1989) and *Pool-e Khareji / Foreign Currency* (1990), revealed a sharp eye for social satire and a sense of solidarity with the underprivileged. The critics recognized a young artist keen on entering the profession of cinema, but they did not find any differentiating features. Scripts written by others did not give her woman's point of view much chance to develop.

With *Nargess* (1992), which she based on research conducted for several years while making documentaries, Bani-Etemad began to focus on adult relationships and problems facing women. *Nargess* begins with images of old photos from a family album and a music box turning the figures of a bride and a groom in a glass jar. The scene is cut abruptly to a man and a woman running from the police. Adel and Afagh are petty criminals fate has thrown together, not a traditional couple like the newly-weds in the glass jar. Afagh, an older woman, has loved and protected Adel for several years, but now he wants to have a 'decent' life, which includes a pure and innocent wife. Afraid of losing Adel, Afagh agrees to ask for the hand of Nargess, a girl from a poor family, pretending she is his mother, on the condition that he will never desert her. After the marriage, Nargess finds out that Adel is a thief and Afagh is not his mother. What shocks her more is the criminal history of Adel. As a good wife, she commits herself to a crusade to lead him to the right path.

The two women are exact opposites, but both are portrayed in a sensitive manner within the triangular configuration. Nargess is young, Afagh has reached a mature age. Nargess is the good woman, the self-sacrificing daughter who left school to take care of her poor family and now wants to reform her husband. Most of the time she is seen with a sky-blue shawl around her. Afagh is the bad woman who swears like a man and smokes. She is a thief who has no intention of repenting. When she comes around to remind the married Adel of his promise not to desert her, she is wearing red, signalling her immoral nature.

Afagh, the thief, is perhaps the first negative woman character of post-revolutionary Iranian cinema, the film provoking regulations that women had to be represented in roles chosen for them by religion, such as dutiful mothers, wives and daughters. Furthermore, the audience is repeatedly reminded that behind her stern façade, there is a real woman with feelings. When she goes to ask for Nargess's hand for Adel, the camera follows her every reaction as she catches the young making eye contact. She offers her own bed to the newly-weds so as not to embarrass Adel in front of Nargess's family with his poor circumstances, but on the nuptial night, her eyes are filled with tears as she reminisces about her better days with Adel. She suffers the pain of abandonment when she sees the wedding shoes of the couple at the door.

Afagh is a woman who suffered a stolen childhood, having been married to a man of fifty when she was only nine. Her husband took away her baby and smeared her name. She has survived on her own on the streets and now she has lost the affection of a man to whom she gave all she had. Her character is definitely much more dramatic than that of Nargess, who represents the ideal woman religion dictates. However, to preserve the sanctity of marriage and restore decency to society, the woman who transgresses must pay with her life at the end. This is what the rules of society and religion (and the heavy hand of censorship) dictate.

Rusariye Abi / The Blue-Veiled (1995) explores the possibilities of forbidden love within the boundaries of societal restrictions. Rasool, a middle-aged, good-natured and rich widower falls in love with Nobar, a very poor young woman who works in his tomato factory. When there is a will, there is a way! Particularly if the hero is as strong-headed as Nobar who refuses to know 'her place'.

The film is very daring for 1990s Iranian cinema, showing in a positive light a relationship that defies customs and religious practices. Additionally, when Bani-Etemad juxtaposes underprivileged women with those from the upper classes, the young factory worker who supports her drug-addicted mother, delinquent brother and younger sister fares much better than the daughters of Rasool who deny their father the chance of starting a new life for fear of losing their inheritance. However, certain points in the film which do not blend well with the rest of the narrative suggest auto-censorship on the part of the filmmaker. For instance, the relationship of Nobar and Rasool is presented as asexual. Concerning the other couple in the film, the worker prefers his wife who grows

Rusariye Abi / The Blue-Veiled by Rakhshan Bani-Etemad (1995) – love forbidden on all grounds

hairs on her face (the harmful effects of hormones in the medical factory where she works) to a beautiful girl his boss wants him to marry. The ending, as in *Nargess* and most likely for the same reasons, also has a moralistic tone. The final scene shows a freight train splitting the frame to separate the lovers.

Despite such details which leave questions in the mind of the audiences, especially those not too familiar with the restrictions that face Iranian filmmakers, Bani Etemad's films display her genuine concerns regarding the lives of young girls who become adults too fast without experiencing childhood, grow too old without experiencing their youth and die too early without experiencing womanhood. The narrative in both *Nargess* and *The Blue-Veiled* is formed from real people she met while shooting her documentaries on the outskirts of Tehran. In fact, these characters seem to haunt her. The protagonist of *The May Lady*, a documentarian like herself,

Banoo-e Ordibehesht /
The May Lady
by Rakhshan
Bani-Etemad (1998)

meets Nobar's sister while working on her new project and questions her about Nobar. She only lived six months with Rasoul, after which his daughters separated them. Now she works in another factory. Nargess, who has custody of her children, still signs petitions to get her husband out of jail and she still has her sky-blue shawl.

The May Lady is about the tribulations of a 42-year-old divorcée caught between motherhood and womanhood in a society where values are constantly changing. The protagonist, Forough Kia, is a filmmaker assigned to make a TV documentary on the subject of the perfect Iranian mother. Her name sets the tone of the story: it brings to mind Forough Farrokzhad, a pioneer filmmaker and a talented poet, something of an Iranian Sylvia Plath and a voice for intellectual Iranian women. The family name Kia evokes homage to Abbas Kiarostami whose films carry a documentary quality.

Forough is a well-educated urban middle-class woman who tries to find her own space between the demands of her lover and the possessive tendencies of her young son. The woman in her yearns for an adult relationship, but such feelings are not well received by her seemingly modern son, who assumes the traditional role of the male head of the family, responsible for protecting the female regardless of her age or status.

We watch Forough and her son Mani go through their daily routines. She is cooking or cleaning nonchalantly while arranging business affairs on the cordless telephone. He is being a typical adolescent, but perhaps not so typical for Iran as we imagine it in the West. This modern boy in blue jeans hangs out with peers and listens to loud rock music in his room, which is decorated not very differently from the room of any middle-class adolescent in the West. He even attends a Western-style party. However, he *is* arrested for his transgression and a patronizing magistrate blames the mother and her divorced status for lack of parental discipline.

The May Lady portrays the life of an intelligent modern woman, a theme which had not been examined so realistically in Iranian cinema before. Forough's interstitial state does not allow her to have a balanced relationship with her son or with her lover. She confides to a friend that a middle-aged woman and a mother cannot speak of love so easily. To declare that she wants to live with the man she loves would entail forgoing the honour of motherhood. In a period of transition from tradition to modernity, the burden is more deeply felt by the women of her social background and status.

In this film, Bani-Etemad effectively solves the problem of the ambivalence created by restrictions imposed on sexual situations in post-revolutionary Iranian cinema by eliminating the male lover totally from the screen space. To display a more natural relationship, she presents him as a voice on the answering machine or a presence in poetic letters. The most commendable aspects of the film are the poetic undertones and the intimate quality of the protagonist's inner monologues.

The opening sequences of the film are significant when we see only half of the face of a woman; the other half is cut by the frame. Later in Forough's bedroom, audience attention is drawn to her photo hanging over the bed; there is a shadow on one side of the face. Is the visible half, the half she shows to the outside world and society, a perfect career woman and a perfect mother, repressing her feelings as a woman? Or is this the half that her son and hence the society are ready to see and accept? Bani Etemad told me during our discussion that the other half, which is not seen, is not limited to personal love. Rather, it is about things she cannot talk about.

The image of a woman with half her face in the dark may also represent the image of women in Iranian cinema, the image that the Islamic Republic has decided to put inside the frame, an image that negates feelings and sexuality and forces women to have a dual character, public and private.

If the film has a weakness, it is in its overall message, which again could be attributed to certain restrictions imposed on filmmakers or to self-censorship. First, there is a tendency

Nun-o-Goldun / Bread and the Vase, a.k.a. *A Moment of Innocence*
by Mohsen Makhmalbaf (1996)

to suggest that the tribulations women face are the same no matter where. This is questionable considering the repressive regime of Islamic Iran. Second, the film shows that all evils that fall on the heads of women come from men. Men beat their wives and throw them out, men run away and leave mothers to shoulder the responsibility of bringing up children on their own, men blame women for not being perfect mothers. In one of the clips from the documentaries of the protagonist, the daughter of the former Iranian President Hashemi Rafsanjani retorts, 'In our country, the problem is the law . . . All judges are men, who don't understand the problems of women.' It is rather simplistic to blame men rather than looking for the roots of evil in the patriarchal system itself. Third, the woman/artist is depicted as a mediator of discordant elements, the balancing force between adverse forces of society. When the son has a row with the militants of the Ansar E-Hizbollah (the followers of the Party of God), his mother, the woman/artist, reconciles the two opposing forces – modernism and fundamentalism – by preaching tolerance and compromise. It is fine to offer flowers instead of guns as in *A Moment of Innocence*, a film by another distinguished Iranian director, Mohsen Makhmalbaf, but the concept is rather romantic for Iran's present reality.

In comparison to Bani-Etemad's subtle and discerning approach to women's predicaments in societies that exercise religious and traditional bias against the female gender, Tahmineh Milani's stand is bold and provocative. Belonging to the generation after Bani-Etemad, she is the most outspoken woman filmmaker in Iran, and is very bitter about the reception she received from the film industry when she first started her career. Male colleagues simply told her to go home, take care of her husband and child and come back later. Determined to say what she had to say at all costs, she made her first film, *Children of Divorce*, without any financial assistance from the authorities.

Milani had difficulty receiving approval for her scripts for different reasons. These ranged from not providing appropriate role models for the youth to designating comic roles for women characters. *Kakado* (1993), a film which raised the issues of environment for children, was ostracized for showing

Tahmineh Milani, Iranian feminist filmmaker

an eight-year-old girl without a headscarf. Milani suggested that the girl was too young to adhere to the laws of the *hejab* (girls are regarded to be mature at the age of nine). Objections were also raised to describing the face of the earth as ugly, when according to the Koran it is supposed to be beautiful. In the ensuing years, all scripts submitted by Milani were rejected by the Ministry of Islamic Guidance.

Following Milani's confrontations with the authorities, a pamphlet called 'Policies and Methods Used in Cinema' was published and distributed among filmmakers. Milani's reaction to the pamphlet was that it must have been written by those who

> could only see black and white. Their mentality does not accept that a woman can say something, be intelligent, be a manager or an educated person, and in

general they have portrayed women as the most isolated, most passive, and most hidden creatures; this means that a woman is nothing . . . Women should not run, there should be no close-ups for women, she should not bend when sitting or getting up, she should never wear make-up . . . They have also defined the roles of women: A faithful wife, a dedicated nurse, and a kind mother . . . they provide it (the model) only for women. It seems that women are dangerous creatures who should be constantly told what they can and cannot do, so that the society can remain safe.[1]

Milani had to wait eight years before the script for *Do Zan / Two Women* (1998) could be approved. Produced during Mohammad Khatami's presidency, it drew over three million viewers in Iran despite the fact that any advertisement of the film on television was banned.

Two Women tells the story of two school friends, intelligent and beautiful Fereshteh from a modest background and the more privileged Roya. (Their names, respectively, mean 'angel' and 'dream' in Farsi.) Fereshteh's student life in Tehran becomes a nightmare when a demented stalker carrying a knife and a vial of acid begins to harass her. Following the Islamist Revolution, when universities are closed for three years, Roya marries a man of her choice and becomes a successful career woman. Fereshteh returns to her small town and marries an older man of means chosen for her by her family. After the marriage, Fereshteh's husband does not keep

Do Zan / Two Women
by Tahmineh Milani
(1998)

his promise to allow her to continue her studies, forbids her to read books, locks the telephone and accuses her of lacking maternal instincts. As her intellectual inferior, he mocks her intelligence and dismisses her desire to study and work outside the home as mere cravings for returning to her 'questionable' living in the big city. When Fereshteh seeks a divorce, the judge asks whether her husband beats her or neglects his duties. The fact that he 'humiliates' her is not a good reason.

Women's right to divorce was restored in late 1983, but mental cruelty does not count as a reason for divorce.

The film's symmetrical structure works on oppositional binarist constructions such as a happily married career woman of average talents versus a socio-economically victimized pretty and intelligent woman; emancipation versus tradition; victim versus perpetrator and female innocence versus male violence. 'Fereshteh and Roya are the same woman,' Milani explained to me during our several discussions in Montreal, Calcutta and Tehran. 'I wanted to show a woman's potential and her reality.' The systematic disintegration of a woman with enormous potential by established conventional forces is very significant. When Fereshteh is finally free of her chains, she cries: 'I feel like a free bird without any wings.'

Fereshteh's ferocious polemics with her father, with the judge at the family court and with her tyrannical husband certainly heighten the dramatic structure and serve as a vehicle for delivering Milani's message. However, the probability of such confrontations is somewhat doubtful. In most patriarchal societies, women are not even allowed to speak in the presence of male authority. Milani defends her position, claiming that Fereshteh is a rebellious character even within her restricted environment. She does not win but she still carries the fight. Iranian women are strong according to Milani. The results of the university entrance examinations are the proof. Fifty-two percent of those who pass are women. The sad reality is that, after graduation, the husband says, 'I don't need your money', and that is it.

The Hidden Half
by Tahmineh Milani
(2001)

All characters in the film are typical characters, Milani asserts. They represent the present atmosphere in her country, but the stalker, specifically, represents bad education. His actions stand as a symbol for living in an atmosphere that trains him to behave in that manner. The violator is also the victim. More than sexual repression, which exists in Iranian society, she explains, his is a problem of identity in a society that does not respect individual identity.

The clear message of the film is that traditional values concerning what makes an ideal woman obstruct the development of a woman's potential abilities, while modern ways of living, such as receiving education and working as a professional, aid her material and spiritual growth. This is perhaps the first time that the oppression of women by men in authority – husbands, fathers or judges – has been so starkly revealed in Iranian cinema. While Milani gained a large number of enemies of the opposite sex, the impact of the film was so strong as to radicalize even 'docile women', as she told me.

Poster for *The Fifth Reaction* by Tahmineh Milani

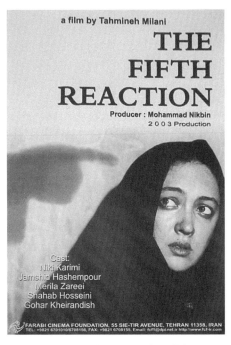

a film by Tahmineh Milani

THE FIFTH REACTION

Producer : Mohammad Nikbin
2 0 0 3 Production

Cast:
Niki Karimi
Jamshid Hashempour
Merila Zareei
Shahab Hosseini
Gohar Kheirandish

FARABI CINEMA FOUNDATION, 55 SIE-TIR AVENUE, TEHRAN 11358, IRAN
TEL: +9821 6701010/6708156, FAX: +9821 6708155, Email: fcf1@dpi.net.ir http://www.fcf-ir.com

Her overt struggle against male oppression did not go unnoticed by the authorities. In the summer of 2001 she was arrested by the hard-line Revolutionary Court of Iran with the charge of insulting Islamic values with her next film, *The Hidden Half*, about a married woman who recalls a romantic love affair with a rebel during the political turmoil of the early 1980s. Milani was accused of slandering the revolution and abusing the arts as a vehicle to express counter-revolutionary sympathies. Although cultural crackdowns often target reformist newspapers and imprison journalists, internationally known filmmakers had been left alone until this incident, partly because they have helped to build a positive image of Iran abroad. Milani was kept in custody for a week and released on bail when President Mohammad Khatami informed the court that her film was authorized by the ministry of culture and, if there was a problem, the government and the minister were the ones to respond.

In 2003, Milani completed the trilogy with *The Fifth Reaction*. '*Two Women* was about the oppression of women in society; *The Hidden Half* voiced their grievances; in *The Fifth Reaction*, a woman comes forward and shows reaction', she told me during the Fajr Film Festival in Tehran. The protagonist is again Fereshteh (always played by talented Niki Karimi), here a recently widowed teacher who fights a desperate battle against her father-in-law for the custody of her children. In a highly dramatic finale, the patriarch makes a concession when he realizes the game is lost in the spiritual sense if not the physical. None the less, he has one condition! (Men always have one condition, says Milani.) Inside the final frame, which is frozen as if to emboss the image in the memory of the audience, the father-in-law points his finger at Fereshteh who is curled up in a corner of a stark prison cell.

Dariush Mehrjui is one of the most accomplished filmmakers of Iran, and earned international recognition in the 1970s with *Gav / The Cow* (1969) which heralded the Iranian New Wave. Mehrjui gained the reputation as a 'women's filmmaker' in the

1990s with films such as *Sara* (1993), *Pari* (1995), *Leila* (1997) and *Bemani* (2002), all of which focus on contemporary women trapped between tradition and modernity. The eponymous heroes are exceptional characters who try to come to terms with their dilemmas in unconventional ways.

Inspired by Ibsen's *A Doll's House* and adapted to Iranian realities, *Sara* presents a positive protagonist, who is effectively involved in the welfare of her family. She saves her husband's life by borrowing the money for his operation without his knowledge and embroiders wedding gowns secretly in the house for four years to pay back the loan. When the husband, who is shown as a self-centred character with tunnel vision, finally finds out, instead of thanking her, he gets upset because now they are indebted to his corrupt clerk. He calls her 'a brainless woman'. In an emotionally charged scene, he stands on top of the stairs and yells at Sara's tiny figure down below that he will not let her bring up *his* child. By the time conflict reaches a resolution, Sara has gained a new outlook on life, which makes it impossible for things to remain the same. Her final look from the rear window of the taxi as she leaves her husband is full of fear and apprehension. The film is open-ended, but there is every indication that her revolt is far from over. Now that she has gained self-respect and confidence, she can have a new start, with or without her husband.

The last duologue between the couple is significant. Unlike the routine conversations about mundane daily matters that we had heard before as the couple sat to eat while watching television, this is the first time they really talk to each other:

Sara by Dariush Mehrjui (1993)

Sara: I have been victimized, first by my father, then by you. Neither of you treated me like a human being. When I was at my father's home, I had to think like him. If I had an idea of my own, I had to shut up because he did not like being contradicted. When I began to see things, I fell into your house. Here I was the mute little darling who had to do what she was told to do and keep quiet.

Husband: No man would sacrifice his honour for the sake of love.

Sara: And yet women do it all the time.

Apart from Sara, there are two other women in the film: the old aunt, who is the epitome of a woman seen and not heard, and Sara's friend and confidante, Sima, an independent, self-supporting widow. Unlike Sara, Sima is not afraid of men. She knows their weak points and she knows how to deal with them, which is unusual for women who are brought up in traditional Muslim households, where mothers install the fear of masculine superiority in their daughters at an earlier age.

Leila by Dariush Mehrjui (1997)

Sara's revolt brings about a revelation; faced with a determined woman, men are as helpless as a child. The roles can easily be reversed. The circular camera shots of the last sequences show the confused state of the husband running around his wife, who is calm and composed as she prepares her luggage. As the taxi pulls away, he stands at the door helpless like a child who has lost his toy. With only a bedsheet covering his lower parts, he also looks rather ridiculous.

Among the 'women' cycle of Mehrjui's work, *Sara* is perhaps the most outstanding. The film enjoyed wide popularity in Iran, especially among women who found the story of a woman's sacrifices for her husband and the selfishness of Muslim men who put disgrace to their honour before everything else very familiar. Mehrjui's stance that oppression of women in patriarchal societies was not exclusive to lower classes was another advantage. *Leila* (1997), also depicting the lives of the more affluent, was much more controversial.

Reza and Leila are a newly-wed modern couple who met each other during a traditional Islamic celebration, *Sholeh Zard Cooking* – an omen that different values are to clash somehow. On her birthday Leila discovers that she is infertile. Intimidated by her manipulative mother-in-law, who possesses all the negative powers that oppressed women in authoritarian societies exercise when they have the chance, Leila agrees to her husband's second marriage and even tries to encourage him. Outwardly, she bows down to tradition but her interior monologues (the voice-over) reveal her torqued emotions about sharing her husband with another woman. This suffering, however, has more than one dimension. Choosing a wife for her husband is also a kind of game for her, a testing ground for the intensity of his love. With each new proposal, their relationship gets closer and more intimate. He showers her with presents. The third time he returns from a 'date', he mischievously says: 'Going to ask for other women's hands in marriage is not all that bad!'

However, when Reza actually marries one of the prospects, Leila feels betrayed and on the nuptial night, runs to her parents' house. Much to the disappointment of the mother-in-law, the second wife bears a girl. Reza divorces the woman he does not love, giving her a large amount of alimony to ease his conscience. After three years and much suffering, Reza and Leila reunite during the same *Sholeh Zard Cooking* celebration. The tradition comes full circle.

Mehrjui attempts to place a distance between the audience and the emotional surcharge of the film by the use of

Brechtian distancing devices. Some characters often talk directly to the camera. However, key episodes, such as the wedding party welcoming Reza's second wife, are shown from the vantage point of Leila so the audience can identify with her dilemma and commiserate with her.

Crucial moments in the narrative take place in gardens with high walls. Three examples are the first meeting of Reza and Leila; the first time the mother-in-law approaches Leila regarding the subject of a second wife; and the reunion of the estranged couple after three years. Although most middle-class gardens in Tehran have high walls, by placing these particular scenes in the confines of such spaces, Mehrjui seems to forewarn the audience about the preservation of traditions within such a milieu. Another device he employs as regards traditions is also significant. The events that comply with tradition are seen but deviations are only heard. For instance, Reza's opposition to his mother's plans for finding him a second wife is revealed through a telephone conversation between Leila and a friend. Leila's only act of defiance, the breaking of the pearl necklace her mother-in-law had given her for 'being a good girl', happens when she is alone in the kitchen. As the preparations for a new wedding progress, she decides to distance herself to cope with her pain and from that moment on, she is framed alone and in shadows.

What is also significant is that men are absent when important decisions are made. Perhaps this is an indication of the hidden power of women inside the family in closed

Muslim societies, although women often resort to devious methods to exercise this power.

Leila was the third biggest box-office hit of the year. Local critics attributed its success to the theme of a selfless wife sacrificing her happiness for the well-being of her husband, which they claimed was very popular in Iranian cinema, serving as a role model for all women. Tahmineh Milani is vehemently against such a representation. She told me *Leila* shows that the husband has the right to take a second wife although he loves his first wife. According to Milani, he does not have such a right. 'The sex of the filmmaker is not so important as what is being expressed in presenting a social problem,' she explained. 'Mehruji is not expressing the problems of women. He is a man who makes films about women; he is not the voice of women.'

Mehruji claims that the situation in *Leila* illustrates the brutal clash between modernity and the Islamic tradition in contemporary Iran where a couple may live in the luxury of modern technology but still accept polygamy. The whole idea is not believable in Leila's situation according to Milani and several other viewers, in Iran and abroad, the majority of whom, not surprisingly, are women.

Bemani / Stay Alive (2002), which incidentally was produced by Tahmineh Milani and her husband Mohammad Nikbin, moves away from middle-class urbanites to the countryside, where the oppression of religion and tradition is tenfold. The film focuses on honour killings and self-immolation, part of the realities of rural life in many patriarchal

Bemani / Stay Alive by Dariush Mehrjui (2001)

Muslim communities. Honour killing, when a woman is killed for her actual or perceived immoral behaviour, is a very common practice in the Muslim world, although there is no sanction of such murders in Islamic religion or law.

The dramatic opening scene of *Bemani* sets the tone as the credits appear over a landscape of barbed wire and a chorus whispers *Salamet* (peace, salvation). A morbid story unfolds in three interlinked episodes around the sad fate of three women.

In the first episode, a young Iranian soldier meets Madineh, a beautiful Iraqi carpet weaver and asks her to weave a carpet for his mother. The romance that develops between the two results in the decapitation of Madineh in the village square by her father and brother to cleanse the family honour.

The second episode begins with the cries of young women students in black chadors at the sight of a human head without the body. Bemani, a teenage girl, stops going to school to take care of her sick mother. As the family is too poor to pay the rent, the girl is forced to marry the rich old land-lord, Khaloo, who treats her worse than his servants.

The third episode is about Nasim, a school friend of Bemani, who has entered the university secretly to study medicine. When her father, a doctor himself, finds out, he humiliates her in front of her classmates, hits her and confines her to the basement for destroying his honour. Nasim sets herself on fire. When Bemani hears about the incident, she runs away to her parents' house and tries to burn herself as well. At the hospital, 'I called her Bemani to stay alive', her father says in tears to the interviewer. Both girls survive. Bemani is rejected by her husband and her family; she leaves town on her own. At a graveyard in the outskirts, she meets an Iran–Iraq war survivor supporting himself by washing bodies. While Bemani is staring at her burnt face in the mirror, the man gives her a carnation and offers her a job selling candles. She will 'stay alive', ironically, among the dead.

The film is based on reports in the newspapers about many incidents of self-immolation occurring in the region of Ilam, where even music is forbidden. Mehrjui uses a distancing device in this film as well: an unseen reporter who tries to find answers to the honour killings and desperate suicides by interviewing people involved.

Despite the tragedy, Mehrjui periodically offers comic relief in small details, such as the scene when Bemani's parents admire the mattress on Khaloo's bed, obviously something they had never seen before. The new son-in-law, although he is the age of Bemani's grandmother, as the old woman justly points out, is respected for having a real home with furniture and two refrigerators in his kitchen. Incidentally, one is his safe, the radar alarm going off every time someone approaches it. The episode when Bemani decides enough is enough and starts beating up her husband and his dog is hyperbolic, burlesque and even surreal, but elicits applause from the audience.

The images of red tomatoes rolling down as Bemani's father hits her for chatting with the shepherd boy or the warm colours of weaving thread that accentuate the flowering of

pure love between Madineh and the soldier, a love that leads
to tragedy, are very striking. The breathtaking countryside
where clear waters gush in total liberty while the villagers
remain imprisoned by their poverty and traditions is testimony to the harsh reality that men have turned against nature
and have created an oppressive world out of paradise.

On the other hand, one may argue that the film is
somewhat too beautiful for its serious subject and such beauty
is often distracting. Something about the way episodes are
linked together does not always work, the editing leaving
certain lapses in the narrative. However, the issue taken up is
an urgent one and Mehrjui should be given credit for exposing such evil doings in the name of 'honour'. The events of
Ilam are not isolated cases, but have their equivalents in other
regions of Iran or other countries where patriarchy rules.
Only women who live in big cities, such as Sara, benefit from
modernization. Amazingly, no one from Turkey, Pakistan or
Bangladesh, where honour killings of women and self-immolation to escape oppression are routine, has yet approached the
subject in such a serious way.

In Turkey, women's issues gained a deeper perspective in the
1980s and began to be considered as a separate genre, paradoxically, with the works of a male filmmaker, Atıf Yılmaz,
who has made countless films with women protagonists. Both
Yılmaz and Mehrjui focus on women, but their films are quite
different. Mehrjui delves deep into the psyche of his characters, searching for psychological or philosophical motivations

Turkish filmmaker, Atıf Yılmaz in front of a work by woman artist Gülsün Karamustafa depicting Türkan Şoray, the star

in their behaviour, and reflects these issues on the screen employing the highest art form available. Yılmaz focuses on the here and now and, by capturing the moment with a keen eye for detail, delivers the best examples of popular cinema.

A close examination of the films of Yılmaz can chart the overall evolution of Turkish cinema regarding women. In the 1960s and 1970s, the general contention was that solutions to social or economic problems would automatically solve problems of women. *Aah Güzel Istanbul / Oh, Beautiful Istanbul* (1966) and *Kuma / The Second Wife* are based on such a premise. In the 1980s, women's issues were regarded as possessing an intrinsic importance independent of other elements. *Mine* (1983), *Bir Yudum Sevgi / A Taste of Love* (1984), *Dul Bir Kadın / A Widow, Adı Vasfiye / Her Name is Vasfiye* (1985) and *Asiye Nasıl Kurtulur? / How Can Asiye Be Saved?* are the best examples of this approach. Beginning with the 1990s, when women, particularly in the urban milieu, liberated themselves from the clutches of tradition and dogmatic religion, marginality and individual sexual choices became the immediate concern. *Düş Gezginleri / Walking After Midnight* (1992), on lesbianism, and *Gece, Melek ve Bizim Çocuklar / The Night,*

Adı Vasfiye / Her Name is Vasfiye
by Atıf Yılmaz (1985)

Gece, Melek ve Bizim Çocuklar / The Night, the Angel and Our Gang by Atıf Yılmaz (1994)

The Angel and Our Gang (1994), about transvestites and male prostitutes, are the best examples of this period.

Kuma / The Second Wife (1974) is one of the landmarks of Yılmaz's career. The film exposes the family structure within feudal relationships, male-child fanaticism and the tradition of *kuma* that allows the husband to take another wife when a woman is infertile or does not produce a male heir. The protagonist Ali bows down to societal pressures and marries a second time when his wife, Hanım, cannot bear children. However, with the gold from Hanım's dowry, he can only pay for a blind woman. While Ali tries to earn money in the city, both wives get pregnant. The blind *kuma* tries to smear the name of the first wife to establish her position, but the city has opened Ali's eyes. In a surprise ending he saves the woman he loves from the clutches of customs and religion that have already branded her a 'whore', and takes her to the big city to start a new life.

The film approaches the tradition of *kuma* in a critical but open fashion, exploring the psychology of the two rival

Kuma / The Second Wife by Atıf Yılmaz (1974)

women with insightful sensitivity. Hanım sacrifices her happiness for the happiness of her man and blind Zilha becomes arrogant and harmful when she endorses her fertility with her pregnancy. Both women are the products of a feudal society and hence believable characters, unlike Mehrjui's infertile Leila, who suffered the same humiliation in her modern bourgeois lifestyle.

Yılmaz returned to the theme of the oppression of rural women by tradition with *Berdel / Bride Barter* (1991), the story of a loving husband who decides to take another wife to have a son after five daughters. As he cannot afford to pay

Berdel / Bride Barter (1991) by Atıf Yılmaz

the *başlık parası* (bride-price), he exchanges his daughter with the daughter of another poor family, a common rural practice called *berdel*. He sacrifices his young daughter to an ill-begotten marriage with an old man with one foot in the grave so that he can have a new wife to satisfy his male-child fanaticism, but receives his lesson when the new wife gives him a daughter while his own wife dies in childbirth bearing his son.

Women's oppression in a society that negates love is the theme of *Mine* (1983), considered a pioneer of films that explore the emotional and sexual needs of women who are prey to pressures of society. Mine, married to a station manager before finishing high school, is very unhappy in the relationship. To add insult to injury, the young and old of the village are obsessed with her sexuality and oppress her with their eyes and obscene remarks. She guards her honour and, despite her hate for her husband, does not have relationships with others. When she falls in love with a stranger, she gives herself to him as an act of rebellion against a society that

Bir Yudum Sevgi / A Taste of Love by Atıf Yılmaz (1984)

denies women their proper place as human beings. The sexual act, which is not shown on screen, is not an end but a beginning; she is not 'dirtied' but cleansed. The final scene, which shows the couple holding hands, stresses the human need for love and understandings.

Love in a loveless society, unhappy marriage, the importance of sexuality and the power of love are explored in *Bir Yudum Sevgi / A Taste of Love* (1984) from a script by Latife Tekin, a woman writer. The focus of the film is the evolution of women in a society that is in transition. Aygül is a young married woman with four children, living in the slums of the big metropolis. She yearns for a man to love her, but her husband is a lazy loser who can hardly stand on his feet. (It is hard to believe that they made four kids together, but that is another matter.) She disdains him and at the same time expects him to fulfil her sexual needs, although every attempt ends in disappointment. As a woman with initiative, she tries to adapt to the constant changes of a society moving towards urbanization and finds a job in the factory, hoping to find individual freedom through economic freedom. She also begins a love affair with co-worker Cemal, who first approaches her as the guardian of her honour. Cemal is also married, and just like Aygül's husband, his wife is dead in bed. They fall in love and after overcoming a number of difficulties (burlesque scenes depicting the clash of opposing forces), get married. The happy ending shows that the magic of love works miracles; the couple is forgiven in the eyes of society.

What makes this film interesting (and highly entertaining) is the way Yılmaz's camera unabashedly intrudes into the lives of the people in the community, exposing the quibbles, eccentricities, weaknesses and joys of characters easily identifiable by the audience. Cemal and Aygül are two very ordinary people. Until they fall in love, they are in situations that bring out the worst in them. Cemal usually returns home late, his sexual need satisfied by his mistress, but he does not hesitate to wake up his wife to ask for *ayran* (buttermilk). Aygül is abusive to her husband, venting her frustrations on her children. True love and understanding change them into sensitive human beings with boundless love to give and receive.

Yılmaz is the first filmmaker to approach the sexuality of the new woman in a positive manner and to create independent women characters. Türkan Şoray, the *sultana* of

Turkish cinema, took her clothes off for the first time in the role of *Mine* and became a new icon. The image of the woman as a sexual being reached its peak with *A Taste of Love*, in the character of Aygül who is neither the gullible virgin nor the sinful prostitute. She is a human being with a right to her sexuality. Both films stress the fact that love is something to be earned and that this needs effort.

The eponymous character of *Mine* is the one who takes the initiative for the first sexual encounter, not her intellectual lover with his typewriter and dreams of becoming an important novelist like Marquez. Aygül also makes all the moves to encourage Cemal, starting with mock-innocent *Cemal Abi* (older brother) to a more flirtatious grabbing of his pen to keep it as a souvenir, writing him a poem (which he reads in the toilet like a teenager in love for the first time). She is shown watching with pleasure the muscular body of Cemal when he plays soccer. She arranges a co-worker's flat to make love and even takes a lesson or two from the 'experienced' neighbour who advises women on sexual matters (such as 'let the man smell but not touch'). During the first physical encounter, the false noises of satisfaction coming from Aygül make Cemal jealous. He wants to know if she has slept with anyone else except her husband. Aygül is very angry that her 'honour' is questioned. Yılmaz never forgets to poke gentle fun at the double standards of men.

The disappointing aspect of both *Mine* and *A Taste of Love* is that they present two choices for women imprisoned in unhappy marriages: accept oppression or try another man.

Düş Gezginleri / Walking After Midnight (1992) by Atıf Yılmaz, the first realistic lesbian film in Turkish cinema

Seeking liberation in individual struggle does not seem to be an alternative for 1980s Turkey.

In the late 1970s, when pornography had its heyday in Turkey, lesbianism was exploited in what were called 'sex comedies', but serious films on the subject did not appear until the early 1990s. Yılmaz is credited for making the first realistic lesbian film in Turkish cinema with *Düş Gezginleri / Walking After Midnight* (1992). He had already experimented with the idea in 1963 with *İki Gemi Yanyana / Two Ships Side by Side*, showing two women kissing each other on the lips, and with *Dul Bir Kadın / A Widow* (1985), about the erotic fantasies of women looking for an identity in a degenerate society who find comfort in each other.[2]

Yılmaz explained to me his motivation for focusing on women in his films:

> The fact that women do not have the same rights as men in Turkey, curiously, makes them more attractive

as dramatic characters; through them one can convey more sharply the problems that face contemporary Turkey. In all levels of society – *Berdel* in a village, *Mine* in a town, *A Taste of Love* in the slums of the city, *A Widow* in high society – women are in a search of an identity. This issue has been resolved in the West, but Turkish society is going through a transition perhaps similar to Iran. *Mine* was the beginning of this search. It came out parallel to the feminist movement of the 1980s and was very successful. A cinema in Anatolia, with a capacity of 200 seats, had to be closed to men, when 190 women showed up. Cinema is an art form for the masses and for that reason, is influenced by the demands of the public, the way the artist is influenced by his environment and the changes in his city. When I make a film, I think of my audience. Traditionally, women have constituted the largest part of the audience in Turkey.

The characters of Yılmaz, be they small-town women, slum dwellers or ambassadors' wives, are very much aware of their sexuality. The bold steps they take to fulfil their desires reward them in positive ways. This aspect sets them apart from the characters in the films of a number of women film-makers, who are often presented as unseemly creatures cut off from their environment. They attain sexual freedom, but not fulfilment. Bilge Olgaç (1940–1994) is the only fully fledged woman filmmaker of Turkish cinema who reflects women's

sensibilities in approaching the realities of women in patriarchal Turkish society.

Olgaç's film career began within the confines of
commercial cinema, Yeşilçam. Her first film, *Üçünüzü de
Mıhlarım / I'll Kill the Three of You* (1965) was a cheap gangster piece with Yılmaz Güney in the lead, killing everyone to
avenge his mother's rape. In the 1970s, when the gangster
genre reached its peak with Güney as its shining star, Olgaç
survived making melodramas, but decided to retire when
Turkish cinema had one of its most serious artistic crisis,
producing almost exclusively cheap sex and adventure fare.

She returned to cinema in 1984 with *Kaşık Düşmanı /
Spoon Enemy* (1984), a black comedy that condemns the sale of
women in the rural milieu. The film is inspired by an actual
event. A gas tube explodes in a house where the women and
children of a village are gathered for a wedding party and
almost all are killed. The focus of the film is the helplessness of
men left without women. Used to sitting in the café all day and
letting the women work in the fields and in the house, they are
not able to perform even the simplest daily chores. In addition,
most of these chores, such as fetching water from the fountain,
are considered too feminine for men. In a society where binary
oppositions are clearly marked, 'manliness' must be guarded at
all costs. Attempts at securing wives from the next village are
not fruitful as the *başlık parası*, the money to be paid to the
girls' families, has risen considerably with the high demand.

In the rural world, women are often called *kaşık
düşmanı*, a derogatory term implying they are economically

unproductive, only another mouth to feed. Olgaç sends a clear message to men of patriarchal Islamic society with this film that exposes women's real position, not only in the aspect of family order and economics but sexuality as well. She is critical of the village men who consider women as merchandise to be bought and sold.

Gülüşan (1985), a love story that blends elements of fantasy and myth within a realistic premise, also examines rural lives locked inside customs and traditions. The film takes place in closed environment: a village house with four characters, one of them blind. Mestan, a worker in the mill has two wives, both of them infertile. He kidnaps a girl he sees on the road, thinking she gave him 'the look'. All he wants is a male child. When he realizes that the girl is blind, he regrets his action and feels hopeless. Then he discovers a special sensuality in the girl. He orders the other two wives to wait on her, which arouses their jealousy. After all, the third *kuma* is also an *eksik etek* (a rural derogatory expression meaning 'women', but suggesting a certain lack). Furthermore, she is blind, which is considered *çürük mal* (rotten merchandise). Products of a feudal system that considers women less worthy than animals, they conspire to crush the weaker one instead of fighting against the oppressor.

Although the film's initial premise is male-child fanaticism, what interests Olgaç more is the suppressed sexuality of a rural man, which can be externalized in the comfort of blindness. As the shame of being naked disappears, through the sensual touch of the blind woman, the macho Mestan becomes a sensitive human being with generous love. However, the portentous black well, standing in the middle of the idyllic garden as a conspicuous trope for feudalism, must devour in its darkness those who deviate from the norm.

Aşkın Kesişme Noktası / The Meeting Point of Love (1990) refutes Laura Mulvey's contention that most films exploit women for 'fetishistic scopophilia'.[3] Long before Jane Campion's camera caressed the naked body of Harvey Keitel in *The Piano*, Olgaç created a flesh-and-blood woman who is physically attracted to a man she sees bathing in the river. The hero, a young widow in the rural milieu, waits for the man to come out so that she can see his naked body. Day by day, she follows him and watches him undress. Unlike Osman of Metin Erksan's *The Well*, who is determined to possess the object of his desire by goodwill or brute force, the young widow chooses to fantasize. She is excited while milking the goat and massages the milk over her skin. She washes herself in an erotic ritual and prepares her body with flowers. When she masturbates, the camera gives her privacy by moving aside to the burning fire, but at the same time, does not shy away from showing images of her beautiful body, not in fragmented images, but as part of a whole, a human being with body and soul. The love scene in the hammock half submerged in the water is very erotic without exploiting the moment of heightened emotions for cheap thrills.

While Atıf Yılmaz tries to expose the issues of women from a woman's point of view, Bilge Olgaç often chooses male characters (except for films of her later years, such as the *Meeting Point of Love*). In *Spoon Enemy*, through clever use of the male point of view, she is able to expose the weaknesses of 'macho' men and satirize their masculinist mentality. In *Gülüşan,* the male protagonist who is the oppressor is equally oppressed. Both films show men's oppression by the established customs, traditions and patriarchal bias of Muslim religion as the driving force behind the oppression of women. The men of *Spoon Enemy* are so entrenched in their ways that one wonders if they learn a lesson from their new experiences, whereas Mestan of *Gülüşan* has the chance to change if his environment could change.

Olgaç, who died alone and poor in a freak accident in her modest flat, burned to death with the reels of her films, once commented that to reconcile being a woman filmmaker in a profession monopolized by men, she had to forget that she was a woman. She tried to make the others forget it too, until they began to feel comfortable enough to swear or fight in her presence. To be able to survive in a male environment, it was very important for her to be seen as one of them.

Zulfikar Mussakov, one of the most productive filmmakers from the younger generation of Uzbek cinema told me during an interview that filmmaking was not an occupation for a woman. Although he admitted that Kamara Kamalova was an exception, his stance was clear. Many women 'lose something from being a woman when they become directors'.

Women filmmakers are rare in Central Asia. To enter the prestigious VIGK (All-Union State Institute of Cinematography in Moscow) was not easy for Kamara Kamalova,

Kamara Kamalova, Uzbek filmmaker

but after graduation, she had to wait ten years before she could find her place in fiction films. She spent this time making cartoons and working in television. In the 1970s, during the Brezhnev era, she set out with determination to create personal films and has become the most prominent woman filmmaker of Uzbekistan.

Atrof Burkanda / Bsjo Vokrug Sasypalo Snnegom / Atrof Qorga Burkandi / All Around Was Covered by Snow (1995) is a surreal love story about a sensitive and strange teenager, Asal, who lives alone in a game reserve. She distrusts people, but feels comfortable with animals of the wilderness. She believes that her mother's death was caused by a ghost who wanders the reserve as a wild dog, which must be killed. Kamil, a hunter who works in the reserve, tries to understand the girl. Soon, Asal's relationship with animals, seasons and nature changes place with the love she feels for a man, and the growing affection between them strengthens her, deeply touching Kamil at the same time.

Atrof Burkanda / All Around was Covered by Snow (1995) by Kamara Kamalova

The film has a very personal narrative style. The feelings of a young girl entering womanhood are explored as she experiences them. Deep emotions, uncertainties and insecurities are articulated through movements, gestures and actions rather than words. Unusually for Central Asian culture, where large families with six to seven children are the norm, Asal has no family. Perhaps this is a symbolic statement about the alienation of youth, particularly during the period of transition following the demise of the Soviet Union, or a metaphor for the independent state itself.

Films with women heroes do not attract much of an audience in Uzbekistan, where traditional patriarchal values are very strong despite long years under the Soviet regime. For instance, Kamalova's *That's Not the Way it Was*, about a strong and intelligent woman scholar, was not successful since the portrayal of such a woman did not please the Uzbek men.

During an interview, Lynne Attwood asked Kamara Kamalova if she had encountered any difficulties because of her gender in becoming a filmmaker. Her answer was a firm 'yes'. Being a director is not only a matter of creativity, but it also involves working with and co-ordinating large numbers of people, mostly men, she explained. Uzbek mentality, which assumes that men are superior to women, does not easily accept women in a position of authority. As for differences between the films made by men and women, Kamalova maintained that some women directors make films as if they have a 'masculine hand', but the fact that women are more sensitive and soft by nature has an effect on their films.[4]

One of the important voices of Kazakh New Wave along with Serik Aprimov, mentioned earlier, Ermek Shinarbaev disrupted the patriarchal order with his first film *Karalisulu / The Mourning Beauty* (1982) by showing that sexual urges also exist for women. A psychological drama, based on a story by one of the most celebrated writers of Kazakh literature, Mukhtar Auezov, the film is about a young nomad widow who takes a vow of chastity that she cannot keep. Written in the 1950s, the subject was considered too scandalous for any director to consider filming until Shinarbaev, a beginner, came along and cast Natal'ya Arinbasarova (the hero of A. Mikhalkov-Konchalovski's *The First Teacher*) in the lead. The film created a scandal, both in Alma Ata (then capital of Kazakhstan) and Moscow. It was denounced as 'un-Kazakh', as Shinarbaev told me in 1991 during our interview in Alma Ata. Even a woman critic, Dilyara Tasbulatova, is harsh on the film:

Karalisu / Mourning Beauty (1982) by Ermek Shinarbaev, starring Natal'ya Arinbasarova as the young nomad widow who could not keep her vow of chastity, was denounced as an 'un-Kazakh film'

She (Arinbasarova) writhes on the bed and mercilessly beats herself, in a literal sense. But the film fails to explore the moral self-flagellation with which this courageous woman coped for a whole seven years – the term of her abstention. The young director, perhaps to his own surprise, made an extremely erotic film, although the original story implied nothing of the sort. Eroticism had been only a metaphor for freedom, and it was not so much the body declaring its rights, but the soul which wanted to break out of the chains of prejudice . . . The problem lies not in the bed scenes themselves. It is much more complex than that. It is funny to see how the ingratiatingly sweet, dull, almost nauseatingly virtuous heroine ends up in bed with some ill-starred actor stubbornly trying to look like a playboy . . . to shoot an erotic scene does not signify that a taboo has been overcome. On the contrary, clumsy eroticism (which borders on pornography) shows more strongly than ever that rough, indifferent and arrogant attitude towards women of which I have already spoken.[5]

Sestra Moia Liussia / My Sister Lucy (1985), partly based on the childhood of the Korean screenwriter Anatoli Kim, is set in a village following World War II. It is a psychological study of two women, a Russian and a Kazakh, forced to live alone. The film evokes problems peculiar to women such as widowhood, parenthood and sexual urges, but at the same time foregrounds the sufferings of humankind, men or women. The scars of war are everywhere. The agony of the wounded soldiers, the humiliation of the maimed young men, the sadness of the orphaned children trying to find comfort in animals and in each other and the desperation of the widowed women forced to sell their husbands' overcoats for a loaf of bread turn the village square into a human gallery. There is an atmosphere of convalescing from a very long illness that has left irreparable damages to both body and soul.

The film juxtaposes two different characters, representing two different cultures. The Muslim woman's suffering is silent and internal, whereas the Russian woman vocalizes her resentment and anger. While the Muslim woman bows her head down to such unjust fate, the Russian woman mocks it. The Muslim woman finds consolation in remaining faithful to her husband's memory despite natural urges. The Russian woman tries to kill the pain inside her, or to punish herself for being alive while another is dead, by humiliating herself in

Sestra Moia Liussia / My Sister Lucy
(1985) by Ermek Shinarbaev

useless sexual encounters. However, the film is not about a good widow and a bad widow. Both women suffer the immutable pain of loss, but deal with it in their own way.

Tasbulatova speaks more favourably of this film, stating that its complex female character, Aigul', the Muslim woman (played by talented Khamar Adambaeva) with an aura of mystery is a relief from the usual pattern of post-war films.

Aigul' is silent almost the entire time, breaking the silence only to make an occasional insignificant remark. So her 'national' qualities – kindness, delicacy and femininity – are not actually declared; the words she speaks are not adequate for this. These qualities emerge, instead, out of the very fabric of the film. Khamar Adambaeva slips imperceptibly into the sequence, moving across the frame, seemingly unaware of her 'Eastern exceptionality'. In short, her performance is not literary, but cinematographic . . . She is Mother, in the highest sense, the faithful Wife, whose husband has not returned from the war, and of course she is a metaphor for all Wives and Mothers. Yet all these various images (each filled with pain) are present in the film in a half-concealed form. They do not lie on the surface. This is mainly thanks to Adambaeva's performance. Her 'elevation to the pedestal' is immersed in daily life. The pathos – if there is any – does not wear on your nerves (probably because it is imperceptible). And if you cry over the sorrows of the women on the screen, your tears are not insincere, they were not squeezed out of you. Aigul' is the first to break the ice of our mistrust towards all these noble heroines – we were so tired of their irreproachability, their coldness and inaccessibility.[6]

A close examination of films focusing on women reveals that differences in approaches are personal rather than genderized. Dariush Mehrjui, a filmmaker deeply concerned with artistic predicaments, finds a niche in women characters that are by nature dramatic figures. Tamineh Milani's predicament is very political. Her characters are crusaders for the rights of women in closed societies. Rakhshan Bani-Etemad, who is also deeply concerned about issues of women, chooses to articulate these concerns through her art. Her characters, regardless of their backgrounds, reveal her feelings, thoughts and experiences as an artist who is very much part of her environment. As a working woman herself, she is aware of the dilemmas of professional and private issues and conscious of thoughts, emotions and sexuality that make up today's Iranian woman. Perhaps she is more successful in projecting these concerns onto the screen than Mehruji, for whom the woman is more of a vehicle to perfect his art.

Critics argue that Atıf Yılmaz is apt in catching certain trends prevalent in society at a specific moment, such as feminism, lesbianism or homosexuality, but does not delve into these issues deeply, that his films reflect photo-story characters and patterns that are synthetic and caricaturized. The fact that he never forgets to put at least one sex scene in each film reinforces the contention that his motivation is purely commercial. In a career spanning over fifty years and involving more than a hundred films, Yılmaz has given Turkish cinema some landmarks that have influenced people and perhaps served as a vehicle to change certain ingrained attitudes in society. One cannot expect all his films to be exceptional artistic achievements. Additionally, their popularity should not be used against them. Compared to some recent art house fare that still retains the old clichés of women as mothers, wives or prostitutes, his films have always been ahead of their time. Furthermore, there is no question as to which side he is on. The same can be said of Ermek Shinarbaev, who shows genuine sensibilities in creating women characters who are very much part of their environment.

5 women heroes of the new iranian cinema

Post-revolutionary Iranian cinema has made its fame in the West with rural films involving children. In most of these highly allegorical stories, the child hero, often a boy, passes through various obstacles to attain human values. Women are filmed in long shots, mostly inactive or in secondary roles.

Films made since the presidency of Mohammad Khatami (1997) display a different picture, as if the film-makers are testing the limits to see how far they can push the relatively relaxed censorship codes. Lauded at international festivals and commercially released in the West, such films focus on women's plight in a period of transition, when traditional values of Islam are challenged by modernity and contemporaneity.

A middle-class adolescent runs away from home when reprimanded for speaking to her boyfriend in the park in Rasoul Sadr-Ameli's *Dokhtari Ba Kafsh-Haye-Katani / The Girl In Sneakers* (1999). Another adolescent chooses to be a single mother in Sadr-Ameli's next film, *Man, Taraneh, Panzdah Sal Darom / I, Taraneh, am Fifteen* (2002). A young woman shaves her head to find work in a weaving sweatshop in rural Iran and is subject to the attention of another young woman in a tale of desperation that ends in tragedy, in Mariam Shahriar's *Dakhtaran-e Khorshid / Daughters of the Sun* (2000). A young bride faces divorce for participating in a bicycle race in Marzieh Meshkini's *Rouzi Ke Zan Shoudam / The Day I Became a Woman* (2000). Women from all walks of life are determined to enter the university at all costs in hopes of changing their status in life in Naser Refaie's *Emtehan / Examination* (2002). Homeless single women roam around Tehran in the dark, seek abortion, do 'favours' to men for money and even prostitute in Jafar Panahi's *Dayareh / The Circle* (2000). Not only do all of these films focus on female characters, but the child heroes of the earlier films have now grown and their difficulties have become more complex. One may say that post-revolutionary Iranian cinema has also reached maturity.

Jafar Panahi focused on the limitations and constraints enforced by society through the eyes of children in his previous award-winning films, *Badkonak-e sedif / The White Balloon* (1995) and *Ayneth / The Mirror* (1997). In his third feature, *Dayereh / The Circle* (2000), he exposes what it means to be a woman in a patriarchal system. The film begins in the darkness of a maternity ward with the screams of a woman giving birth and ends in the darkness of prison where terrified women huddle together for solidarity. The screams heard in the opening sequences could be coming from a torture chamber until the voice of the nurse announces the birth to a

above: Badkonak-e sedif / The White Balloon (1995)
by Jafar Panahi

right: Jafar Panahi in front of the poster of *Dayareh /
The Circle* during the Rotterdam International Film
Festival 2001

silhouette in black chador. At the end, it becomes evident that
the maternity ward was actually inside the prison. Between
these equally depressing places, which are both linked to the
world outside with a small window, young women run around
in circles.

Dayareh / The Circle (2000)
by Jafar Panahi

Solmaz (which ironically means a flower that does not fade) faces rejection by her in-laws for giving birth to a girl. Nargess (meaning 'daffodil'), a vulnerable country girl with a purple bruise under her left eye, dreams of returning to her village, which she believes is depicted in a Van Gogh painting she saw in the marketplace. Arezou ('wish' in Farsi) does not have the courage to accompany Nargess, in case her paradise does not exist. Pari ('fairy' in Farsi) is pregnant with the child of an executed man. Trying to enter her father's home, she is chased away by her two brothers. Elham, an ex-cellmate who has now married a Pakistani doctor, refuses to help Pari, fearing that any connection with a prison inmate would reveal her secret past to her doctor husband and endanger her status as a respectable married woman. Another ex-prisoner sells tickets at a cinema. She gave up her rights to motherhood for the benefit of her children when her husband remarried during her confinement. She is even thankful to the second wife for looking after them. A single mother abandons her little girl in desperation and is arrested for soliciting when she accepts an invitation to get in the car of an elderly driver who happens to be the chief of the *komiteh mobarezeh ba monkerat,* Committee Against Immorality. A prostitute with a disillusioned smile on her heavily made-up lips is arrested while her client goes free. To the question of the *komiteh* chief as to why she is doing this, she answers with another question: 'Are you going to pay for my keep?' A car passes by carrying a newly-wed couple, the woman's face hidden behind her bridal veil. The prostitute follows the car with her eyes, the expression on her face not giving away whether she is envious of the woman in white or derisive of the tradition that forces women to hide their faces even in their assumedly happy moments.

The women in Panahi's *The Circle* are not allowed to travel alone, to check into a hotel or to smoke in public. They have to be invisible to exist in a world dominated by men. They are in constant state of panic, hiding behind cars, in dark alleys and under their black *chadors*. Their destitute attempts to have a puff of smoke, a motif that is repeated several times in the film, becomes a metaphor for all the freedoms that are denied to their sex. When the prostitute stares unabashedly at her male jailers and lights a cigarette on her way to prison, her defiance has the impact of a heroic declaration of freedom, which speaks for all oppressed women.

'The prostitute can stand for all the other characters that end up in a dead-end situation. The difference is that she has accepted the reality about society whereas the others are still searching for an open door out of the vicious circle', Panahi explained to me in 2002 at the Rotterdam International Film Festival:

Each character that I introduce, in a linear progression, displays a higher degree of experience and a more profound, yet disillusioned, view of life. Nargess is idealistic in her naiveté. For her, the painting of Van Gogh evokes memories of a beautiful place. Then again, art should have that quality to evoke hope! Arezou, who has been hardened by the blows of life, has lost her faith in paradises where problems do not exist. Society has trapped all of these women in a circle. Their attempts at getting out of the circle resemble a relay race. If one of them succeeds, they all succeed, but if one fails, they all fail.

Panahi does not want to limit the *impasse* situation the film espouses to the circumstances of the Iranian society, or to the situations of women in patriarchal regimes and traditions. 'Everyone lives in a circle', he asserts, 'the reasons can be economic, political, cultural or familial. In my films, I try not to put the blame on a particular person, male or female, policeman or soldier. Each person is a human being with innate goodness. Societal differences cause problems.'

The film exposes a new picture of Tehran, from the perspective of outcast women, which has not been so daringly explored before. The open challenge to the social system is more political in *The Circle* than in Panahi's two previous films. One may argue that abortion, prostitution, family violence and abandonment of children are universal issues not unique to Iran. However, in the closed society depicted in the film, women are the recipients of the blame and the bearers of the burden. Men seem to be freer to do as they please. Over a telephone conversation, we hear that one of the revolutionary guards is having an affair with a married woman, an act not likely to put him behind bars but, under the laws of *sharia*, a woman can be stoned to death for such transgression. Morality squads target prostitutes and not their clients. As Panahi admits, 'the radius of the circle is larger for men in Iran'. The screams heard in the opening sequences show the urgent need to express pain and to put an end to silence in order to bring about change.

The Circle, which won the Golden Lion at the Venice Film Festival, 2000, encountered several difficulties with Iranian censorship, as was expected. Moreover, it has been criticized by many Iranians, both inside and outside of the country, for not being true to life, for catering to occidental expectations, or for depicting the issues of only a certain segment of society, namely lower-class women. Although Panahi admits that to accentuate the restrictions faced by women he had to go into the poor districts of the southern part of Tehran and among a social class where limitations are more visible, he believes that whether you are privileged or not, the laws are the same.

'I wanted to raise the question right in the beginning as to why there must be so much sadness when a girl is born', he explained to me:

In the remaining 86 minutes of the film, I talk about other restrictions these girls will face. Originally, I intended to begin the film with the guards naming the three girls coming out of prison. However, fifteen days before shooting the film, I had doubts about that scene. Then I remembered an incident: When I was a student, the day I was presenting my theses, my wife gave birth. I ran to the hospital and found out she had a daughter. The first woman I saw was my mother. She said, 'Jafar, don't worry, it is not a shame, but you have a daughter.' Even my mother wanted me to have a son despite the fact that I already had a son. The moment of birth is the moment that establishes the difficulties of a woman's life; it symbolizes it.

At the end of *The Circle* Elham, who has chosen to live with the burden of a hidden past, is the only woman who remains out of jail, which does not mean she has escaped the circle; rather precariously, she is hanging on it somewhere. Officially integrated to society through marriage, she is not free to make any decisions or to exist without her husband. How long can she remain there and on which side she would slip are open-ended questions. The implication is that those who hide their true self, or an important part of their lives, behind a protective mask are the survivors, although the mask they wear may estrange them from their friends and from themselves. It is not incidental that Tahmineh Milani called her film about a middle-class wife who wants to face her husband with the secrets of her political past, *The Hidden Half.*

Women's issues have always been controversial in post-revolutionary Iranian cinema and served as borders not to be crossed. However, in the last few years, despite difficulties encountered by Milani and some others, an unprecedented number of films dealing with the plight of women in a patriarchal society have reached occidental audiences, a phenomenon often attributed to the moderate regime of President Khatami.

Panahi does not agree that there are more films on women's issues today than in previous years. 'Well-known filmmakers such as Bahram Beyza'i or Dariush Mehrjui have often attacked the subject and women directors such as Rakhshan Bani Etemad and Tahmineh Milani have consistently made films about women's problems', he pointed out.

> I would not say that there is a new trend about women's films. Established women directors have become more established and the young ones have come and begun to tackle issues close to them. Evidently, if you have a more open regime, you dare more, but this is one reason among many. Each year between sixty to seventy films are produced in Iran. Among these, there are films about women's issues. Commercial films that lack artistic merit do not draw as much attention. They treat a social problem as it has always been treated – before and after the Revolution. Discrimination arises from the quality of the films rather than the subject matter. In my first films, I worked with children and

young people but I began to think of the limitations facing these girls once they grow up. As I was increasingly interested in acute social problems, I had to get away from the child's point of view. The characters have grown up and their difficulties have become more sophisticated, which needed to be expressed in stronger statements.

The Girl in Sneakers is the story of a teenager trying to escape her monotonous middle-class existence to experience individual freedom, a common occurrence in modern occidental lifestyles, which, until recently, had not been openly acknowledged in traditional and religious societies. The runaway youths have become a serious menace to the Islamic Republic of Iran. Many of them hang out in the parks, at the railway or bus stations, vulnerable to drugs, prostitution or rape; girls often shave their heads to look like boys to avoid problems.

Rasoul Sadr-Ameli, an ex-journalist, based his film on an actual event. Fifteen-year-old Tadayi takes long walks in the park with a like-minded boy called Aideen. They share their thoughts and dreams and envisage a future life together somewhere far away from parental authority. Such an innocent act is considered a transgression under the Islamic law that forbids unrelated underage couples to be together unchaperoned. At the police station, the two families accuse each other of a lack of responsibility towards their offspring, and Tadayi's parents force her to undergo a virginity test. The

Dokhatari ba Kafsh-haye-katani / The Girl in Sneakers (1999) by Rasoul Sadr-Ameli

routine manner the doctors and nurses in the hospital deal with the issue is a testimony to the fact that such tests are not rare. Hurt by the humiliation, Tadayi skips school and keeps calling Aideen for some assurance, but his parents do not let her speak to him. Watching movies to kill time, she is late meeting her father. When she spots him talking to a police officer, she runs away. After dozing off in a park, she is woken by a poor boy, Naseem, who sells sweets. Naseem's mother, Mahpareh, takes Tadayi to the shantytown where they live. Harassed by some lecherous rough men, Tadayi escapes with Mahpareh chasing after her. With the help of Mahpareh's boyfriend, Tadayi has a chance to meet Aideen again in the park, although Mahpareh, hardened by life, has a premonition that this reunion will only lead to disappointment. Aideen's father had a frank talk with the boy about the realities of life (which he should have done earlier to avoid the entire hassle, the film seems to insinuate). Standing in the cold park, which looks unfriendly and menacing in the dark, seems irrational to him when he can be in his comfortable bed. It is so much easier to conform to the rules of society. Tadayi bitterly places the flower of the unconsummated wedding that was to take place among strangers on her hair as she realizes that all that talk about flying to far away places was just talk. After two days of an exhausting journey through the city, she ends up knocking on her parents' door.

Tadayi is not much different from any teenager of her class in any part of the world. Her room is messy; her clothes have an air of rebellion to discipline and authority; and her general attitude reveals the precarious nature of her transition from childhood to adulthood. She hates walking on the paved road, opting for walking on kerbstones. She prefers to be able to choose rather than follow a path chosen for her. The white sneakers she wears could be taken as symbolizing her pure and independent spirit. However, her protected existence as a middle-class teenager has left her too naïve about the realities of society. When she steps to the other side and experiences a life that is in sharp contrast to her secure environment, she is lost.

Mahpareh dopes a rented baby to carry on her back so that she can handle illegal stuff inconspicuously. She is a survivor. 'There isn't even an insect related to me in the city', she says. People of the slums live by their own rules in a constant battle for survival. They have no scruples about stealing children to rent them out to beggars and thieves. At the outset, their precarious lives appear more colourful and adventurous than the routine of a middle-class home, but Tadayi must return to where she belongs, where there is security, symbolized by the lights turning on in the living room as she rings the doorbell.

The theme of the alienation of youth, which is central to the film, is established through the opening shots in the park as the camera accentuates the verticality of the motionless trees, juxtaposing their firm permanency with Tadayi's horizontal move in society. The audience familiar with Iranian cinema may interpret the fact that Tadayi is played by a completely unknown actress, whereas the adult roles are played by familiar faces as an endorsement of this theme.

Despite its smooth direction, attention to detail and particularly the heart-rending performance of the young female actor who plays Tadayi, certain problems, which may have their source in governmental censorship policies, self-censorship on the part of the director, or simply the director's personal convictions, leave question marks. Ameli treats the issue of runaway adolescents as a social problem, but avoids getting too close to his characters as if to ward off the danger of some impressionable youth identifying with them. Tadayi's exhausting odyssey brings her face to face with alterity, be it a subterranean culture or subterraneous side of otherwise upright moralists, yet she is not shown as reaching a self-awareness from this experience.

A close reading of the film reveals a systematic deliverance of moral guidance from an authoritative voice:

Lesson Number One: Don't trust boys! They don't mean what they say even if it may sound like they mean it when they say it. Mahpareh warns Tadayi that 'it is not enough to be from uptown, there is no woman who can't be fooled'. Aideen's change of heart proves her right.

Lesson Number Two: Don't trust older men, especially the uncle types! They are lecherous wolves. The middle-aged man she meets on the street sounds sympathetic to her grievances and even throws in a moral or two, but turns out to have indecent intentions.

Lesson Number Three: A girl alone (without a male owner/guardian, father, brother, fiancé) is in constant danger. All men are potential threats. She may be taken for a prostitute and coerced into getting into strangers' cars, or treated without respect even by insignificant hotel clerks and waiters. Outcasts who live in the periphery of society, including women, pose a serious threat. Mahpareh's initial reaction to the run-away girl is to sell her or ask for a ransom. 'Surely some bastard will show up for her anyway. Whoever pays more, they are welcome to her', she tells her boyfriend.

There are lessons for the adults, too. Tadayi tries to reach out to people she trusts, but they disappoint her. Her married cousin Azadi is too busy with her cooking to listen to Tadayi when she calls her. Her Grade Two teacher, who does not really remember her, thinks she should be ashamed of herself to say at her age that she is bored and tired. In one of her adventures, a rather humorous episode takes place on a bus. A number of middle-aged women first eye her suspiciously, but later commiserate with her when she makes up a story about having leukaemia. Should the young have leukaemia to be noticed, Sadr-Ameli seems to be asking.

Parents are warned to pay more attention to the needs of their kids although the parents in question look very regular, doing what their class and social standing would do under such circumstances – namely doing their 'duty'. When trouble arises, the father blames the mother since, within traditional Islamic culture, to raise the children is the duty of the mother. The man works himself to death and this is what he gets! When mother tells the father that months pass and he never asks about his daughter, he says, 'Do I have to baby-sit, too?'

The mother displays concern when she brings food to Tadayi, who is grounded in her room after the incident with the police, but it is evident that she is in complicity with her husband. The girl shows no emotion when her mother takes off the gold chain of her own mother from her neck and gives it to her. Is this a silent apology for the demeaning way she was dragged to the hospital for the virginity test; a reward for being found a virgin; or a bribe to be good in the future? Her moment of defiance comes when she tries to pawn the chain to survive on her own.

Tadayi's lament to a stranger is significant as it sums up the double standards modern middle-class urbanites must adopt to survive in an authoritarian society. 'My parents do what they want, but in secret. They are always worried about what people might say. They dress differently at home, outside or at parties. They say we must be careful of our reputation.' Interestingly, the stranger, an upright-looking middle-aged man who delivers the right answer to every question, turns out to be the epitome of double standards, revealing a subtle cynicism of authority on the part of the director.

Daring in its subject, *The Girl in Sneakers* nonetheless endorses the status quo, the middle-class values of closed societies. After wandering the streets for some days and nights (and miraculously nothing bad happening to her), Tadayi returns to the safety of her home. She won't run away again! There is no place to go for a girl who runs away. The film tries to offer a balance between unlimited social freedom and extreme restrictions. The underlying message is that unlimited freedom is not fit for a society that is not ready for it.

If an unmarried couple can be arrested for simply walking together in public in the restrictive Islamic society of Iran, surviving as a single mother is practically out of question. The protagonist of Sadr-Ameli's next feature, *Man, Taraneh, Panzdah Sal Darom / I, Taraneh, am Fifteen* (2002) chooses the hard way. According to the film, her situation is not so uncommon as one thinks.

In *The Girl in Sneakers* Mahpareh, the outcast, tells Tadayi that she is just an impressionable middle-class kid who cries when she is in real trouble. With her mother dead and her father in prison, Taraneh is not so naïve, hence, this film

*Man, Taraneh Panzdah Sal Darom /
I, Taraneh, am Fifteen* (2002) by
Rasoul Sadr-Ameli

is more daring in presenting a more mature teenager who is determined to raise her baby alone. Furthermore, at the end of the film, she gets what she wants.

Taraneh lives with her grandmother and works part-time in a photo shop. At school, she receives the model student award for being responsible for her life. She visits her father regularly, bringing him presents and even her poems. There seem to be love and harmony between the two.

Her troubles start when Amir, a middle-class boy working in the carpet shop next door, begins to take her photos. Afraid to lose her job in disgrace, she tries to avert the boy's attention by telling him their lives are different. Amir is to go to Germany to join his father who is divorced from his mother, but he wants to marry Taraneh and stay in Iran. His mother proposes *sigheh* (temporary marriage) until they finish their studies, hoping secretly that the infatuation will not last.[1] 'That way they won't have problems in public places', she says. Taraneh's grandmother warns her that she will only be a common wife, but her father gives his consent, as he only wants to see his daughter happy. Four months later, Amir is arrested in the company of three women not related to him, a crime according to the Islamic Civil Law. His excuse to Tareneh is that he is tired because she never wants to go out. Taraneh does not answer.

The next time she visits her father, she tells him that she will seek divorce. During the divorce proceedings, his mother tells the judge that the girl needs a responsible person and her son is not responsible. 'It was only an intimacy pronouncement so that he does not commit a sin if he sees your hair, your leg, or if you hold each other's hands', she says to Taraneh in front of the judge. After the divorce, Amir is sent to Germany and Taraneh finds out that she is pregnant. Amir's mother suggests an abortion, but Taraneh decides to keep the baby. She has an early delivery. To get an ID in the name of the father proves to be difficult. Amir's mother refuses to acknowledge her son's paternity and a long struggle ensues. Taraneh wins the case but decides to give the baby her name, which is her way of recovering the dignity she has lost.

Interestingly, the motif of youth as the potential inno-cent victim of a hypocritical authority figure in *The Girl in Sneakers* also appears here in the role of the mother-in-law whose job as a social worker is to aid women in difficulty. When her interests are at stake, she is the one creating the difficulties. The temporary marriage is her idea, relying on her son's immaturity for the relationship to be short-lived. She tries her best to get rid of Taraneh, including finding a potential husband for her.

It would not be far fetched to read the tribulations of the women heroes of *The Girl* and *I, Taraneh* with authority figures as an allusion to the difficulties the young generation, particularly the women, face in Iran in their struggle to assert their individuality. After tasting temporary freedom, Tadayi accepts the societal restrictions as inevitable and returns home, whereas Taraneh defies the imposed mores of religion and tradition and exercises her right to freedom of choice. Rather than seeking an abortion and burying her unfortunate experience behind a shroud – choosing denial – she prefers the hard road of single parenthood. Her action is in contrast to the character of Elham, in Panahi's *The Circle*, who can survive inside the vicious circle drawn by forces mightier than the individual only through denial. Iranian youths of the twenty-first century have passed the stage of chasing impossible dreams of freedom and are now ready to act on it. The demonstrations that erupted in June 2003 are evidence to their determination to take an active role in their future.

A different reading may interpret Taraneh's decision to keep her baby as a moral one: the film invariably praises the qualities of spiritual growth and motherhood. The girl is an exemplary student, a devoted daughter and a caring grand-

daughter; a perfect role model for youth. Choosing an irre-
sponsible partner and getting pregnant at a very young age
changes her life as a respectable young woman with a future to
being a social outcast subject to discrimination, humiliation
and loneliness. Her single status bothers the neighbours, who
keep an eye on the comings and goings. In fact, a prostitute
she meets in the park shows amazement that she could get a
flat at all, 'in a neighbourhood with three mosques'.

When faced with the choice of having an abortion or
keeping her baby, she chooses the second road, which is more
difficult, but 'honourable'. The prostitute advises her to get
rid of her baby. 'It is easy to find a few fools in the bazaar to
tell them it is their baby to get some money', she explains. One
of her friends even bought a mobile phone with the leftover
cash from her abortion. Taraneh's moral rectitude and developing mother instincts cannot tolerate such comments. Self-
righteously, she tells the prostitute to leave, as if the woman
would contaminate her little nest with her impure thoughts.
Such moralistic naïveté ignores the fact that all women who
have abortions are not prostitutes and that it takes more than
a loving mother with good intentions to bring up a child.

Furthermore, the plausibility of the absence of evil or
evil thoughts in the film is open to discussion. Taraneh comes
to terms with the fact that Amir is not for her, but she does not
bear any grudge against the boy who was arrested with three
women while they were still married, and continues his care-
free life while she has to wait on tables with her big belly. She
accepts her situation without inner conflict and tries to deal

with it without bitterness and without pessimism. During a particular scene in the cafeteria where she works, the camera focuses on youth presented as degenerate and invites the audience to identify with the one who is 'Islamically correct', that is, Tareneh, who accepts hardships and humiliation to bring a human being into the world.

Just like *The Girl in Sneakers*, despite modern characters and controversial subject matter, *I, Taraneh* also conforms to the rules of the long-term plan for cinema set in the years following the Islamic Revolution by showing the triumph of self-sacrifice and decency over selfish and immoral behaviour. Its happy ending, which has now become a cliché in Iranian social cinema, endorses the unquestionable belief in the supremacy of moral good. However, one has to consider the censorship context before judging the message of the film as ambivalent. To show an unwed teenage mother, prostitutes who ply their trade in the park and a social worker favouring abortion already make this film ahead of its time.

In Naser Refaie's first feature, *Emtehan / Examination*, young women choose higher education as a means to enlarge the radius of their circle, if not as an exit door. However, the chances of success are very slim: only one-tenth will pass the entrance exam and, even if they have a university degree, they will most likely end up jobless.

The film begins with a long shot of a big iron gate. Girls in black chadors arrive, on the back of a motorcycle driven by a man, in a Mercedes driven by a woman, with their fiancés, husbands, babies or alone.

To pass the time, the upper-middle-class girls talk about beauty and nose-jobs and, with urban superiority, tease the guard, a country boy. Young men wearing dark sunglasses sit on the hoods of their cars or cruise for girls. A father whose sense of morality is disturbed by the scene starts a fight, disregarding the pleas of his embarrassed daughter. A woman tries to console her friend with a bruised eye: 'If I get married and he does this, I would set him on fire', says she. 'You will learn to be patient after you get married', is the answer from the battered woman. A husband is raging because his wife came to take the exam without telling him. He told her before marriage: 'University or me!' 'You can't even have control over your wife.' Some women think something is wrong with a woman who does not obey her husband. A mother is busy seeking a nice wife for her son. An old woman says she tolerated her husband for seventeen years but finally she put an end to it all. The response from the young is that there is no choice. 'Divorced women are worse and if she marries again and the next one is the same, she has to kill herself.'

Refaie employs a multi-layered approach to display a large spectrum of people. In each part of the film, the camera zooms in on several new faces, like eavesdropping, and after a few seconds, moves to other newcomers and then returns as if to catch up where it left off. Ostensibly random episodes are choreographed to reveal, on the one hand, the hopes and ambitions of women, their actual and desired places in society and, on the other, the fundamental assumptions of an androcentric religious culture regarding women. Young women consider higher education as a vehicle to improve their status in life even if they may not find jobs at graduation. 'The university exam is like an upside down funnel', one girl comments. However, husbands, fathers and even mothers consider female schooling unnecessary and even threatening to the sanctity of marriage. A pompous young man remarks that 'Some women who get educated think they are better than their husbands, so they separate.'

Choosing a situation where people with the same goal are gathered on the same route, Refaie tries to expose individual differences in a society that expects uniformity from all of its citizens. You can put on a black chador and make everyone look alike, but you cannot kill individuality, he seems to be saying. Different people have different characters, lifestyles, aspirations and needs, which are often determined by social and economical conditions. For a woman in a wheelchair with no prospects of marriage, 'a girl is either pretty, or goes to university'. For the one whose parents are ready to marry her off to the first man, education is a pretext to avoid an unwanted marriage. All women, wearing the black chador – of uniformity – are in the same situation of waiting to take the step that could make drastic changes in their lives, but each one arrives with her own set of life experiences. Whether they succeed or not, the outcome will not be the same for all.

For rural women with limited resources, education is beyond dreams. *Dakhtaran-e Khorshid / Daughters of the Sun* (2000), the first feature of woman filmmaker Mariam Shahriar, begins with the long black hair of Amangol, a pretty village girl, falling ritually to earth and scattering in the wind. Three younger girls watch in silence. Long shots of the countryside reveal a bleak image of barrenness and destitution. When the camera returns to the girl in a close-up, her head is shaved. She shoulders her bundle and leaves in boy's clothes. A sad Azeri love song is heard as Amangol, who will from now on be called Aman, approaches another destitute village that is announced by electric poles that appear as the road gets larger. A bicycle passes by with a languid girl of Aman's age side-saddled behind a man.

The owner of the sweatshop is surprised that the fragile new 'boy' is an excellent weaver. He puts her in charge of the three girls who sit on a separate bench. As a supervisor, she is flogged whenever something goes wrong. Locked inside the cell-like workshop every night, with only a hand now and then appearing to deliver food and no one to share her secret, Aman begins to lose her sense of reality. She even promises Belgheis, the young woman who is in love with her, that they will marry and settle in her village. Pressured into marrying an old man, Belgheis hangs herself when Aman retracts the marriage proposal. The news of the death of her mother is the last blow for Aman, who, with silent deliberation, douses the sweatshop with gasoline and sets it on fire. Donning her full skirt, she takes the road with the same Azeri love song that was heard in the beginning. The camera follows her triumphant walk away from her bondage, feminine to the core while the barren landscape gradually gains colour. The government officer for employment and security who has

Dakhtaaran-e Khorshid / Daughters of the Sun (2002) by Maryam Shahriar. Silence as the only weapon against male oppression

been looking for the village all along finally arrives while the smoke from the burning sweatshop obscures the miserable village as if it never existed.

Aman's fate is little different from the fates of many girls from destitute families who are sent off to work as boys. Majid Majidi's acclaimed *Baran / Rain* also depicts an adolescent girl dressed as a boy who replaces her wounded father on a construction site. However, in that film, Latif falls in love with Baran only after he discovers her true identity and even then, his is a spiritual love that does not seek earthly rewards. With *Daughters of the Sun*, UCLA graduate Shahriar challenges the cinematic restrictions in several ways; showing an actor with her head shaven and bare is the most obvious one. However, eliminating around fifteen minutes of dialogue and replacing it with some obscure long shots to circumvent censorship have created certain ambiguities, resulting in an elliptic film with a narrative that relies heavily on visual decoding.

Baran / Rain (2001)
by Majid Majidi

No longer a woman to the outside world and not a man in her inner feelings, Aman bears the burden of her dual personality in silence, often wavering between her attraction to the itinerant *saz* player and her co-worker, Belgheis. In a rather surreal scene, with the unexpected opening of the bolted door, the *saz* player offers Aman the chance to escape, but she does not dare. The presence of the itinerant *saz* player who seems to have a magic touch is somewhat numinous. Aman's dervish-like whirling around her cell with her long skirts carries pretersensual mysticism. The manner in which the camera captures this intimate moment through the open window, which was barred all along, brings an oneiric quality to the experience. Yet it also creates noncohesion, as it does not link well with other, similar episodes.

Furthermore, and perhaps for obvious reasons, whether this man and this woman are aware of Aman's real identity is not clear, although occidental audiences, zealous to read between the lines in any film coming from restrictive regimes, have already labelled *Daughters* 'Iran's first lesbian film'.

More important than its transsexual innuendos, the film delivers urgent warnings regarding the problematic status of women in a masculinist society. The opening scene when Amangol's father cuts her hair, a trope for her identity, is symbolic of the way women are forced by male authority figures, be they representatives of the state or heads of the family, to give up their femininity by hiding it behind black curtains. Condemned to an existence without a voice, silence becomes the only weapon for women against oppression. This is the silence of Keje in *Seyyit Han* (Güney) who meets death without uttering a word to the man she loves, or Berivan in *The Herd* (Zeki Ökten), who accepts violence (both physical and emotional), but remains doggedly silent. Silence also serves as a powerful metaphor in this film. The long takes of the earlier scenes establish a desolate landscape where the silence of the arid earth is nearly palpable. In a tiny cell with an earth floor, women are shut in silence and at the mercy of a man who values his horse more than human beings. Amangol's particular situation not only exposes her to abjection but also condemns her to deafening silence.

The film is very pessimistic about the future of young women, especially in the underprivileged rural milieu. However, Shahriar offers a way out of the vicious circle, no matter how drastic it may be. The direct message to thousands of oppressed women is 'Man brought you here; it is up to you to get out. Don't wait to be saved, save yourself!' When Amangol douses the sweatshop in gasoline, one can almost hear the audience applauding.

Rouzi Ke Zan Shoudam / The Day I Became a Woman, the first film of Marziyeh Meshkini (wife of the acclaimed filmmaker Mohsen Makhmalbaf) is a sequential triptych that charts the kind of life a woman born in a traditional culture can expect. Each part of the triptych has a different title, which serves as an allegory as well as a name to the hero. In the first part, *Hava* (referring to Eve or the first woman), a girl wakes up on her ninth birthday and finds out that she is now considered a woman. 'I woke up a woman today, is it true?' she asks a little boy with whom she can no longer play. According to tradition, which is still strong in rural areas, from that day on, she will be restricted from certain actions and places and obliged to wear the *hejab*. In the second part, *Ahoo* (meaning 'deer', a beautiful but wild animal), a young woman who joins a bicycle race is chased by her husband on horseback with threats of divorce if she does not quit. When she refuses to comply and continues to pedal determinedly, she endures public humiliation from the males of her clan. In the third part, *Hoora* (meaning a beautiful woman with dark eyes), an old woman who no longer has the chance to recapture her lost childhood and youth tries to live out her dreams through the accumulation of material objects.

Little Hava faces restrictions from her mother and grandmother regarding playing with the boys or wearing what she wants, which shows how customs that have become ingrained over time hamper women's freedom. Havva tries to have fun playing on the beach, but when the appointed time for her passage to adulthood arrives, she must bow down and give up her freedom. Her mother and grandmother, chador-clad women entrusted with the continuation of custom, are ready to throw the black chador over her head. In fact, the manner in which they measure the fabric to get it ready is little different than preparations for a coffin. For women born into fundament-alist societies, there is no escape from the assigned female role.

The second story focuses on men's role in the oppression of women by customs and religious traditions. Ahoo's husband tries to restrict his wife's freedom in the name of the clan and God. Her struggle to escape her imposed condition is symbolized through her determination to pedal non-stop, knowing too well that eventually, she will be caught. At times, her doggedness has a playful edge to it. The bicycle race of two dozen women in chadors is a very strong metaphor. As fast as they pedal, they know very well that there is no place to go; they are surrounded by the sea. The little girl has not had a chance to enjoy her childhood and now her youth is also denied to her.

Hoora represents the older generation; she was not allowed to enjoy her childhood and not allowed to develop individuality in her youth. Now it is too late to recapture lost moments. Her emotional hunger can only be satiated by worldly acquisitions. She has bought everything she could buy, from household appliances to luxury items. Local boys help her cart her goods to the seaside, to embark on a voyage to an undisclosed destination. Then she goes back to buy more. In a Felliniesque scene, the boys raid the refrigerator placed on the sand, and have fun turning on all the appliances even though there are no electric plugs. Then the old woman takes to the sea on a raft with all her acquisitions. The black flag on the mast suggests death as the only answer to freedom for women, but the sea may also serve as a refuge for Hoora to preserve her dreams.

Hoora is the old age of Havva and Ahoo. She is the mixture of modernism and tradition, which clash. In the first part, the grandmother of Havva has difficulty with the clock, so she gives the girl a stick to measure time. In the second part, a bicycle is a problem for Ahoo's husband and the rest of the clan, who are on horseback. In the third part, an old woman has neither a husband nor family to restrict her actions, but she has no possibilities either. Her youth is gone, so is her beauty. She is financially equipped to buy whatever she had desired in the past, but a thread on her finger, tied for remembering the goods to be bought, still remains. All the money in the world cannot buy her lost youth and her dreams.

According to Meshkini, despite the bleak picture it displays as to the fate of women in closed societies, the film is not without hope. At the end of the second part, the camera follows Ahoo's emotional struggle on her bicycle in a tight frame, then suddenly pulls away and pans to the sea leaving the end open to interpretation. There is a bird flying towards Ahoo, which may suggest freedom for all the Ahoos of the world.

Movement promises change. 'The situation one is trapped can be changed by movement . . . I want to say that a movement has started and should continue – like a river that flows non-stop. The movement of the women is the movement of the river. It is a metaphor. They are progressing to reach their final goal which is freedom', asserts Meshkini.[2]

Panahi is not so optimistic. At the end of *The Circle*, the girls go back to prison. 'They have enlarged the circle, but they cannot come out of it', Panahi reiterates. 'I don't know to what extent the fact that these girls run away or the fact that I make this film can change society. They may raise questions about attitudes, but to change the laws is much more difficult. Only history, time and social reforms that may and may not come will prove whether this film has had an impact.'

afterword

A close look at the film industries examined in this book reveals that there is no lack of women in their films. Women are always present, even if their presentation may not have any significance. Often, they are presented to be 'seen'. Very few films are about women 'seeing'.

Despite their improved juridical position, women experience the paradox of false modernity in many Muslim countries. They are not yet considered free individuals but still as belonging to a family, which thinks and decides on their behalf and acts accordingly. Film industries that are run by men carry the same patronizing attitude towards women.

Conflict between tradition and modernity is nothing new. The issue has gained a new dimension in the Islamic countries with the recent marked visibility of women, even where their vision is subject to veiling.

Paradoxically, the most progressive films about women are made in Iran where *sharia* rules every aspect of life and cinema. Sceptics may call feminism and Islam an oxymoron. However, the struggles of committed filmmakers such as

Tahmineh Milani, among others, have led the way to a more daring cinema and the films from the younger generation discussed in Chapter 5 are the proof. A movement has started, as claimed by Meshkini. The works presented in this book, from Iran and elsewhere, suggest that the direction this movement will take will be determined by the new generation.

references

introduction

1 Edward W. Said, *Covering Islam* (New York, 1981), p. 127.

1 representations of women

1 ... *Ve kadınlar*
  Bizim kadınlarımız
  Korkunç ve mübarek elleri
  ince küçük çeneleri, kocaman gözleriyle
  anamız,
  avradımız, yarimiz,
  ve sanki hiç yaşamamış gibi ölen
  ve soframyız daki yeri
  öküzümüzden sonra gelen
  ve dağlara kaçırıp, uğrunda hapis yattığımız,
  ve ekinde, tütünde, odunda ve pazardaki,
  ve karasapana koşulan
  ve ağıllarda
  ışıltısında yere saplı bıçakların
  oynak ağır kalçaları ve zilleriyle bizim olan

> *kadınlar*
>
> *bizim kadınlarımız.*

From Nazım Hikmet, *Memleketimden Insan Manzaraları: Kurtuluş Savaşı Destanı / Human Landscapes from My Country: The Epic of Liberation War* (Istanbul,1965), pp. 59–60. Translation by the author.

2 Georges Bataille, *Eroticism* (London, 2001), p. 133.
3 Chidananda Das Gupta, *The Painted Face: Studies in India's Popular Cinema* (New Delhi, 1991), p. 146.
4 Bahman Maghsoudlu, *Iranian Cinema* (New York, 1987).
5 Tanvir Mokammel, 'Last Two and Half Decades of Bangladesh Cinema: In Search of an Identity', *Celluloid*, xx/3 (1998), pp. 30–34.
6 Lynne Attwood, ed., *Red Women on the Silver Screen: Soviet Women and Cinema from the Beginning to the End of the Communist Era* (London, 1993), pp. 187–8.
7 Yılmaz Güney, *Yol* (Istanbul, 1994), pp. 241–2. Translation by the author.
8 Roy Armes, *Third World Film Making and the West* (London, 1987), p. 275.
9 Güney, *Yol*, pp. 275–328. Translation by the author.
10 Pierre Bourdieu, *Masculine Domination* (Cambridge, 2001), pp. 50–51.
11 Krishna Sen, *Indonesian Cinema* (London and New Jersey, 1994), pp. 51–2.
12 Attwood, ed., *Red Women*, pp. 190–96.

2 violence against women and the politics of rape

1 Pierre Bourdieu, *Masculine Domination* (Cambridge, 2001), pp. 52–3.
2 Chidananda Das Gupta, *The Painted Face: Studies in India's Popular Cinema* (New Delhi, 1991), p. 163.
3 Lynne Attwood, ed., *Red Women on the Silver Screen* (London, 1993), p. 128.
4 Karl G. Heider, *Indonesian Cinema: National Culture on Screen* (Honolulu, 1991), p. 67.

3 islamist cinema as a genre

1 Deniz Kandiyoti and Ayşe Saktanber, eds, *Fragments of Culture: Everyday Life in Modern Turkey* (London and New York, 2002), p. 263.
2 Nijat Özön, *Sinema Uygulayımı Tarihi* (Istanbul, 1985).
3 Ziba Mir-Hosseini, 'Iranian Cinema: Art, Society and the State', *Middle East Report*, 219 (Summer 2001).
4 'Iranian Cinema Today, Trust, Not Suspicion', *Film International*, V/3 & 4 (1998), pp. 6–7.

4 women's films, films about women

1 'As Restless as her Characters: An Interview with Tahmineh Milani', *Film International*, V/2 (1997), pp. 48–53.
2 One of the earliest films to display (closet) lesbianism is *Haremde Dört Kadın / Four Women in the Harem* by Halit Refiğ, which was attacked by fundamentalists, who destroyed the reels during its screening at the Antalya Film Festival of 1966, declaring the film an insult to the Turkish family.

3 Laura Mulvey, 'Visual Pleasure and Narrative Cinema', *Screen*, v/3 (Autumn, 1975).

4 Lynne Attwood, ed., *Red Women on the Silver Screen* (London, 1993), p. 232.

5 Ibid., pp. 188–9.

6 Ibid., pp. 189–90.

5   women heroes of the new iranian cinema

1 According to Iranian custom, there are two types of marriage: permanent and *sigheh,* temporary. Temporary marriage gives some sexual freedom to divorced women, but even a virgin can have a temporary marriage. Children of such unions are legitimate and entitled to a share of the father's inheritance. As women are expected to be virgins when they marry, temporary marriage is not respected by society. However, clerics, officials and even feminists discuss it as a solution to the problems of youth.

2 Jahanbakhsh Nouraei, 'Movement is Symbol of Life', *Film International*, VIII/1 (2000), pp. 25–8.

select bibliography

Dabashi, Hamid, *Close Up – Iranian Cinema: Past, Present and Future* (London and New York, 2001)

Kazmi, Nikhat, *The Dream Merchants of Bollywood* (New Delhi, 1998)

Mernissi, Fatema, *Islam and Democracy: Fear of the Modern World* (Cambridge, MA, 2002)

Mir-Hosseini, Ziba, *Islam and Gender, The Religious Debate in Contemporary Iran* (Princeton, NJ, 1999)

Ramusack, Barbara N. and Sharon Sievers, *Women in Asia: Restoring Women to History* (Bloomington and Indianapolis, 1999)

Saktanber, Ayşe, *Living Islam: Women, Religion and the Politicization of Culture in Turkey* ((London and New York, 2002)

Saliba, Therese, Carolyn Allen, and Judith A. Howard, eds, *Gender, Politics and Islam* (Chicago and London, 2002)

Schulze, Reinhard, *A Modern History of the Islamic World* (London and New York, 2002)

Tapper, Richard, ed., *The New Iranian Cinema: Politics, Representation and Identity* (London and New York, 2002)

films and addresses

Useful details for some of the films discussed in this book:

bangladesh

Lalsalu / A Tree without Roots by Tanvir Mokammel
Kino Eye Films
45, Central Road
Dhaka 1205, Bangladesh
e-mail: tanvmel@bol-online.com

kazakhstan

The films of Ermek Shinarbaev
0618288657@mailbox.kz

The Last Stop by Serik Aprimov
Distributor: Arkeion, Paris
Fax: 33 45 22 73 50

uzbekistan

Uzbekkino
98, Uzbekistansky prospect
Tashkent 700027, Uzbekistan

india

National Film Development Corporation
www.nfdcindia.com
Film and Television Institute of India (Pune)

Mere Mehboob / *My Sweet Love*
Hyphen films
101 Wardour St
London WIF OUN
nmk@hyphenfilms.com

indonesia

Directorate for Film and Video Development
(Ministry of Information)
Jalan Merdeka Barat 9
Jakarta, Indonesia

Sri by Marselli Sumarno
Fakultas Film dan Televisi-Institut Kesenian Jakarta
Jalan Cikini Raya 73 Jakarta 10330 Indonesia

iran

Farabi Cinema Foundation
75, SieTir ave.
Tehran 11358, Iran
fcf1@dpi.net.ir
www.fcf-ir.com

malaysia

The National Film Development
Corporation of Malaysia
Studio Merdeka Complex
Lot 1662, Hulu Kelang
68000 Selangor D.E., Malaysia

pakistan

Khamosh Pani / Silent Waters by Sabiha Sumar
World sales: Les Films du Losange
22 avenue Pierre 1er de Serbie
75116 Paris, France
d.elstner@filmsdulosange.fr
www.filmsdulosange.fr

turkey

Turkish Republic Ministry of Culture,
Directorate General of Copyrights and Cinema
Kızılelma Mah. Anafartalar Cad. No:67
06250 Ulus, Ankara, Turkey
kultur@kultur.gov.tr
www.telifhaklari.gen.tr

acknowledgements

I would like to express my gratitude to filmmakers Zeki Demirkubuz, Tanvir Mokammel, Ermek Shinarbaev, Ali Özgentürk and Atıf Yılmaz; producer Kadri Yurdatap; professors Oliver Leaman, Oğuz Makal and Semire Ruken Öztürk; Farabi Cinema Foundation and its general director Amir Esfandiari; Ankara Flying Broom Women's Film Festival and producer and author Nasreen Munni Kabir for their support and assistance; and to Phyllis Katrapani, filmmaker and my daughter, for her encouragement and intellectual criticism.

photo acknowledgements

I would like to thank Farabi Cinema Foundation in Iran; *Cumhuriyet*, a Turkish daily newspaper; Istanbul Foundation for Culture and Arts and International Istanbul Film Festival; and filmmakers Tanvir Mokammel and Ermek Shinarbaev for providing stills for this book from their archives. The two stills from *Baran / Rain* reproduced on page 180 are courtesy Miramax Films. The portrait photographs reproduced on pages 104, 115, 132, 146 and 157 (bottom) were taken by me.

index